Contents

Leading FaithHome for Parents Groups

Welcome to FaithHome for Parents resources. We hope that this study guide to the faithhome booklets will offer a successful learning experience for the parents in your congregation.

These study sessions can be used in:

- Sunday school
- Small Group sessions
- Parenting Seminars
- Family retreats
- Women's or Men's Groups

Each class can be completed forty-five minutes. If more class time is available, leaders can allow more discussion and sharing.

What you'll need

This book offers a step-by-step guide for leading sessions with 12 FaithHome booklets. This guide includes the text from each booklet for easy reference for the leader.

For each class, you'll also need a FaithHome booklet for each parent or couple. Because they are sold separately, by topic, you'll only need the booklets for the sessions you choose to teach. There is a list of all FaithHome booklet topics, inside the back cover.

For parents who would like to read more, each booklet lists additional books and resources. For more information on the series, visit the website at www.FaithHome.com

For a successful class

One of the benefits of learning in a group is the sharing and support from other parents. Sometimes parents will hear a new idea or learn from parents with older children. Most often, reassurance comes from hearing that other families, particularly in their church, have problems like their own.

For the sessions to be most beneficial, everyone in the group needs to feel comfortable talking about their family. They will need to feel assured that the stories and concerns shared will be kept confidential. You may want to consider a Group Covenant affirming the group's commitment to support and privacy.

Next Steps

If your group would like to continue study with more focus on the age of their children, two other FaithHome studies are available. *Talking with Your Child: Conversations for Life* and *Talking with Your Teen: Conversations for Life*. Each offers a leader's guide and a parent handbook.

Communicating with Your Preschooler

Learn the art of truly talking with your child

FaithHome for Parents

Gathering Time
(6-8 minutes)

On a table at the front or in the center of the room, display several children's books (from your family's collection, the church library or public library). Choose books appropriate for different ages: a cloth book with a different texture on each page, an alphabet book, a story book, a picture book. Choose books that are old favorites for young children, and one or two that may be new.

As participants arrive, encourage them to compare notes on their own children's tastes in stories, and exchange storytime experiences.

Prayer
Call the group together with a word of welcome and begin with this prayer or
your own:

O God, You spoke and worlds were created. You spoke Your will through the prophets. When You wanted to communicate Your love to us You did it through your Word, made flesh. Thank You for these good parents who want to grow and learn to be better parents. Help all of us to embody Your love and grace as we communicate with our children, in Jesus' name, Amen.

Scripture
(1-2 minutes)
Read aloud the Scripture (Mark 10:13-14) printed on page 7 in the booklet.

Say:
You communicate with your child all the time, whether you realize it or not. You communicate love, appreciation, tension, impatience, distraction, and many other messages in the way you look, speak, listen, respond, touch, and move. On the other side of the equation, your child communicates with you too, first through crying, then coos and gurgles, laughter and tantrums, and--haltingly at first, and sometimes comically--with words.

In this session, we will learn to communicate more effectively with our preschoolers.

Scenario
(3-4 minutes)

Read the scenario from the booklet (the story printed in italics).

Rosemary, age four, accompanied her parents to a gathering in memory of a friend's father. Many of the family and other adults there were very sad and openly cried or shared stories about the father and grandfather they had lost. As the adults were talking, Rosemary said, "My grandfather died too. We were really sad."

On the way home, Rosemary's dad asked her how she felt about what she had seen and heard. He also asked her about what she had said about her grandfather. Actually, Rosemary's grandfather was alive and well and living in Texas.

Preschoolers have many ideas and feelings they do not know how to express verbally. Young preschoolers, who do not have the words to explain their feelings, generally act them out. Older preschoolers, like Rosemary, have limited vocabularies and often tell stories or fantasies to get their ideas across. As a parent, understanding how your child communicates is an important step in building good communication. Encouraging healthy and open conversations with your young child now is important because the first five years of his or her life are a crucial period for the development of self-esteem, confidence, and a sense of being part of the world in which he or she lives.

Ages and Stages
Although all children are continually developing their communication skills, there are specific changes or abilities that can be observed around each birthday. Every child is different, and some progress more rapidly than others, but common stages include the following:

Two-year-olds
Two-year-olds can understand and sometimes talk about things that can be seen and touched. Converse with your child about these things, even when the conversation is one-sided. Your child will be able to respond more and more as you continue the conversations. The more you talk with your two-year-old, the better. Realize that two-year-olds are experiencing increasing frustrations as they want to do more and more things for themselves but aren't able.

2

Three-year-olds

Children this age are beginning to have opinions. Give your child plenty of opportunities to express those opinions by asking him or her "yes" or "no" questions. Then progress to simple questions such as, "Who is here to see you?" or "Which of these two do you like best?" Begin to "mirror" or to describe and name your child's emotions. Say, without criticizing, "You're really mad," or "That scared you, didn't it?" If you can help your child identify feelings with words, such as *mad* or *sad*, he or she can begin to say these words instead of acting out the feelings.

Four-year-olds

As your child becomes more capable of expressing thoughts and feelings, encourage him or her to talk in short but complete sentences. Respond to your four-year-old in a similar way.

Five-year-olds

Five-year-olds are beginning to discern simple emotions and are able to talk about activities that happened over time. Encourage your child to tell you about his or her morning, teacher, favorite foods, and so forth.

These language development characteristics have an important implication for you as a parent: You should communicate with your child in age-appropriate ways. Remember that using baby talk is not necessary for preschoolers to comprehend the message. Young children understand more than they are able to communicate.

Hints for Improving Communication with Your Preschooler

1. Find time to communicate with your child. Our busy lives—with hectic schedules for both parents and children—often leave little time for conversations between parent and child. In fact, less time for parent-child interaction is the most significant hindrance to building communication with our children today. Less time means less opportunity to praise and encourage our children's first attempts to express their feelings through language. As parents, we must be cre-

Ask:
Did Rosemary tell a lie?
What do you think she was feeling?
What do you think she was trying to communicate?

Ages and Stages
(8-10 minutes)
Summarize the developmental skills of the various age levels, reminding the class that these are average levels of progress. Individual children may be ahead or behind this stage at the same age. [Note: Parents may disagree with these stages based on their own child's experience. That's okay, but discourage comparisons or competition.]

Hints for Improving Communication

(8-10 minutes)

Take time to discuss each of these ideas. Be sure to allow for discussion in this section; these tips may generate other ideas from the class.

Writing the four main ideas on a board or newsprint as you go may help structure the discussion and keep you on target:

1. Find time
   ▲ Praise attempts to express themselves
   ▲ Look for opportunities in everyday routine
   ▲ Use signs and landmarks during car travel
   ▲ Set aside 15 minutes as daily time with your child.
2. Try different ways to converse
   ▲ Talk about feelings
   ▲ Talk about simple sights, sounds, smells
   ▲ Offer choices
   ▲ Repetition
   ▲ Use manners

ative in finding time to communicate with our children. Here are a few ideas to try:

▲ Be aware of opportunities for talking to and with your preschooler while you're "on the go"—driving in the car, working or playing around the house, or even walking from the car to the grocery store.

▲ While you're out and about, talk with your preschooler about the many different signs he or she sees. Make it fun by teaching your child to identify and name signs for the grocery store, hospital, toy store, and other familiar places in your community.

▲ Set aside at least fifteen minutes each day as uninterrupted time for you and your child to talk about the day. If you can, arrange to spend this time together at the same time every day. Your child will begin to look forward to this ritual.

2. Try different ways to foster communication and conversation:

▲ Talk about moments from your child's day, such as what made him or her happy, sad, afraid, or mad.

▲ Talk about concrete things in your child's world, including sights, sounds, smells, colors, and textures. This is a fun way to help your preschooler learn to communicate his or her thoughts.

▲ Offer choices. Try saying, "Would you like a hot dog or soup?" instead of "What would you like to eat?" When helping your child get dressed, say, "Will you wear the red outfit or the blue one?" Although offering choices is important, be sure to limit the choices to two. Offering too many choices or asking a broad question is overwhelming to a young child.

▲ Ask your child to repeat any instructions that he or she does not understand. This verifies communication and assists with sequencing, listening, and language development. Keep in mind that preschoolers cannot remember a series of instructions.

▲ Demonstrate appropriate manners with your own language. Encourage your child to say "Excuse me," "Please," "Thank you," and "I'm sorry" when appropriate. These phrases can be learned as soon as your child has developed a working vocabulary.

4

3. Use "conversation alternatives" to encourage communication and build a connection with your child.

▲ Sit with your child at bedtime as he or she prays aloud. You can learn a great deal about your child's daily thoughts and fears by listening to his or her prayers. This is a good quiet time for asking questions and offering reassurances.

▲ Playing simple games or singing age-appropriate songs gives you and your child time for back and forth conversation.

▲ Reading together is an excellent way to help build communication together, especially if you talk about the story. Try asking your child to describe what is happening in the picture and what might happen next. Even before he or she can read, ask your child to take the book and tell you the story. You will learn what ideas and perceptions are in your child's mind. When your child is old enough, have him or her read to you.

▲ Even nonverbal actions can foster communication. Reassuring looks and gestures will help your child feel you are interested in his or her thoughts and feelings.

4. Talk to your child about fears. Preschool children often have fears about what they can't control, such as the dark and thunder. They don't have the words to explain their fears, so they often make up stories. They may be afraid of monsters under the bed, or other fantasies, when their real fear is being alone at night. The story may not be real, but your child's fear is very real. Here are some helpful hints for discussing your child's fears:

▲ Do not dismiss your child by saying that the monster isn't real or there's nothing to be afraid of.

▲ Ask questions such as "When does the monster come out?" and "What does the monster look like?" to better understand what your child is really afraid of. Your child may be transferring fears of the dark to monsters, or anxiety about a particular family problem to loud noises or storms.

▲ Give your child helps for handling the fear. For example, ask if monsters melt with light and then give your child a flashlight, or try

5

3. Use alternatives to conversation
   ▲ Prayers
   ▲ Games
   ▲ Reading
   ▲ Non verbal activities
4. Talk about fears
   ▲ Don't dismiss fears
   ▲ Ask questions
   ▲ Offer help

Conversation Stoppers

(8-10 minutes)

These no-no's may need a little explanation.

Over-explaining: Don't give the child more than he asks for. Remember the dad who responded to "Where did I come from?" with the birds and bees speech. When he finished, his son said, "Oh. Joey came from New Jersey." Sometimes a simple "yes" or "no" is enough.

Exaggerating: Words like always and never are "nag words," and most probably untrue, as in "You always leave your toys out, and you never pick them up!"

Shaming: Telling a child he is bad or stupid is a powerful parental message that sticks in his mind forever.

Frequent interruptions: Interrupting is rude no matter who does it. Also, don't answer for your child. Allowing her to talk and answer for herself is good practice and affirms her status as a person of worth.

Non-verbal signals: Children are acutely attuned to body language setting a "monster trap." Anything you can do to understand the underlying fear and offer your child a feeling of power will help your child to deal with the anxiety.

Conversation Stoppers

▲ Over-explaining. Keep ideas simple, concrete, and concise.
▲ Exaggerating. Exaggeration confuses rather than adds emphasis for a child.
▲ Shaming. Using negative labels and names when correcting a child shuts down open communication. Correct your child clearly and appropriately for the behavior. Remember that positively affirming the desired behavior when giving instructions is a more effective way to communicate with your child than reminding him or her of bad behaviors.
▲ Frequent interruptions. Often young children have trouble getting to the end of the sentence, repeating and restarting the same thought again and again. It's tempting to finish the sentence for them! As often as possible, try to give your child time to finish.
▲ Nonverbal signals. Even when you're not speaking to your child, you are "communicating." Impatient gestures, signs of tension, and angry facial expressions may be telling your child more than you suspect.

When to Seek Help

It is important to remember that all children develop at a different pace. Some begin to talk early and have a 300-word vocabulary by age two-and-a-half. Others barely do more than make the simplest noises until age three. Even so, if you feel that your preschooler is not responding to you or to his or her environment, you may want to have your child's hearing and/or speech tested. You may need to investigate a preliminary test if your child

▲ does not respond to his or her name unless you are making eye contact.
▲ does not react to loud noises, even when they are in close range.
▲ consistently struggles to articulate simple words, particularly those with beginning or ending consonants.
▲ continues baby talk after age five.

6

Regardless of your child's communication abilities, remember that his or her world is filled with teachable moments. Enjoy these years when your child wants to communicate, needs to learn how to share thoughts and feelings, and is still connected to you in a way that provides many opportunities for discussing the unknown and the unseen. Appreciate the innocence in your child's voice, the glisten in your child's eyes, and the wonderment of your child's mind. These are the days when you can freely communicate your love for your child and see and feel reciprocated warmth.

The Faith Perspective
Mark 10:13-14

People were bringing little children to him in order that he might touch them; and the disciples spoke sternly to them. But when Jesus saw this, he was indignant and said to them, "Let the little children come to me; do not stop them; for it is to such as these that the kingdom of God belongs." (NRSV)

Children learn and listen best when snuggled on a lap where the touch of nearness and security grounds them. Secure in the arms of love they can then see, hear, and quickly grasp ideas and words from the wider world. The Bible paints a clear picture of how deeply Jesus understood the hearts and minds of children. He wanted them to touch him and crowd around him with sticky fingers, shy smiles, and zany questions. When adults tried to straighten the kids up, Jesus got angry and said, "Stop! Let them come as they are. Let them crawl on my lap. Let them touch and explore and ask me to tell my stories again and again. These small ones are full of wonder. They sit at the center of life in my kingdom." The best we can do for our children is to gather our children close, retell the stories of Jesus, and let them handle Jesus with hand, heart, and mind. Your kids, like those for thousands of years, will want to come close to Jesus.

Think back to your childhood. Did you have a favorite Bible story? Retell it to your children today and include why it meant so much to you. Act it out. Draw a picture of it. Make up a song about it. With hand, heart, and mind introduce your kids to the Jesus you know.

7

and tone of voice. They know, sometimes before you do, when you are tired or cranky or tense.

When to Seek Help
(1-2 minutes)
Briefly mention each of these indications that perhaps speech or hearing should be tested.

The Faith Perspective
(4-5 minutes)
[If you have a picture, painting, or statue that depicts the scene of Jesus and the children, have it available.]
Re-read the Scripture that you read at the beginning. Then read the section of the booklet text that describes the scene in modern language.

Say:
Jesus knew about communicating with kids. He knew that touch and closeness are as important as what you say. Most of all, he knew--and taught--that every child is a Very Important Person.

Your assignment:
Tonight, take a few minutes before bedtime to tell a favorite Bible story. Ask

your child what his favorite Bible story is. Let him tell it to you.

Closing
(2-4 minutes)
Ask for any questions or thoughts.

Close with this prayer or one of your own:

O God, great Giver of all gifts, You gave us the wonderful gift of children. Grant us also loving hearts and the wisdom to communicate our love to them. Give us ears to hear what they would say to us, and keep our own words gentle, for Jesus' sake. Amen.

Recommended Resources
Books That Build Character: A Guide to Teaching Your Child Moral Values Through Stories, by William Kilpatrick and Gregory and Suzanne M. Wolfe (Simon & Schuster, 1994).
God's Love is Like. . ., by Ray Buckley (Abingdon Press, 1998).
My Many Colored Days, by Dr. Seuss, (Knopf, 1998).
1001 Things to do with Your Kids, by Caryl Waller Krueger (Abingdon Press, 1988).

For more resources visit www.FaithHome.com.

About the Authors
D. Tony Rankin parents with his wife, Amber. They have three children: Drew, Caleb, and Katelin. When he's not parenting, coaching baseball, or dancing with his daughter at her recitals, he is the director and clinical therapist of The Counseling Center in Nashville, Tennessee. In addition to numerous advice columns and magazine articles, he is the author of *When True Love Doesn't Wait.* He enjoys speaking at seminars and conventions and has taught as an adjunct instructor in psychology and religion at Belmont University.

Cynthia Ezell is a licensed marriage and family therapist in private practice in Nashville, Tennessee. She is also a certified Imago Relationship therapist and a certified group psychotherapist. She is the author of "Growing Up," a monthly column on parenting appearing in *Nashville Parent* magazine. She is the proud mother of three daughters.

FaithHome for Parents provides the church community with resources to support families and help children *to increase their faith, confirm their hope, and perfect them in love.*

ISBN 068708886-0

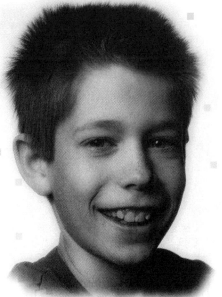

Communicating
with Your
Child
Ages 6-12

Learn the Art of Truly
Talking with Your Child

Gathering Time
(5 minutes)

Write on a chalkboard or large piece of paper this statement: "A parent's job is to work himself or herself out of a job." As class members arrive invite them to join in discussing what they think that means. You may choose to do this in groups of two or three or with the group as a whole.

Prayer

Begin with this prayer or one of your own:

Gracious God, thank you for the miracle of life, and especially for the wonder of childhood. Make us mindful of the trust you have placed in our hands by the gift of these children. Help us to take delight in them as we guide them toward you. We ask this prayer remembering that we are all your children, in the name of Christ. Amen

Read the Scripture from page 7 of the booklet (I Samuel 1:27-28).

Scenario

(4 minutes)

Read the scenario from the booklet (the story printed in italics).

Ask:

Does this sound familiar? In what ways are your children like the four described here?

Say:

As your child moves out of the sphere of home and family into the world of school and friends, your parenting role and your child's needs change. You may be the "home port," but your child is learning to navigate in new territory. Even as peers exert strong influence, parents are still extremely important teachers and role models.

Maintaining Good Communication

(8-10 minutes)

Read the first sentence in this section ("The main developmental task..."). Have the class name a few of the tasks a 6-12 year old can do for himself that a preschooler cannot.

Say:

This is part of the reason this period is often called "the golden age"; the dependency of the pre-

---

Beth and Daphne are sitting on the school's playground swings discussing who they think is the cutest boy in their class. As they giggle, they chit-chat about who's talking to whom, who's in the club and who's not, and other things about school, scout group, and church.

Jimmy and J.T. banter back and forth about whose baseball team is the best and which of them runs the fastest. In the midst of the friendly debate, they discuss the most recent price increases in the new baseball card magazine.

The parents of these four children marvel at the changes in their communication abilities since kindergarten. The children want to be seen as "included" and successful, and they compare themselves constantly to their peers. Beth and Daphne are very concerned about the social pecking order—who is popular and who is not. Jimmy and J.T. are very interested in sports performance and grades. All of their parents wonder whether or not they understand how to respond to their changing children.

Why Is Maintaining Good Communication Important Now?

The main developmental task or job of children ages six to twelve is to be able to do things for themselves. This period of a child's life often is called "the golden age." Children have the cognitive skill to process and think through ideas but do not yet need to separate from their parents. Your goal during these years is to help your child explore his or her world, make good choices, and feel competent and successful.

Open, active communication during your child's elementary years is especially important for several reasons:

▲ Building a habit of honest, open communication now will lay a good foundation for adolescence, when your child's will and the problems he or she experiences will require more trust and more of a connection with you.

▲ Your discipline of your child during these years is more likely to be based on reasoning and the negotiation of privileges. The goal of your discipline is to help your child learn to make good choices, and this age is the best time to help your child learn to make better decisions. Your child is mentally able to weigh options and is still interested in your opinion.

2

▲ You may be spending less time with your child as school and social activities become a bigger part of his or her life. Though you may have less time together, you are still an extremely important social model for your child. Your child returns from his or her world with a lot of information to process and many stories to tell.

Hints for Improving Communication with Your Child

The three main communication issues with children in the elementary years are security, predictability, and responsibility. Let's consider each of these important issues and some of the things you can do to give your child the reassurance, support, and guidance he or she needs:

1. Security. Tell your child how safe he or she is, and explain the types of protections that are in place to ensure that safety. Reassure your child regularly of your love.

2. Predictability. Stay as consistent as possible in your language, expectations, and schedules. Having structure and knowing what to expect are important for children this age.

3. Responsibility. Begin to help your child be responsible for his or her words and actions. Take the lead by demonstrating that your "yes" means "yes" and your "no" means "no."

Here are some other helpful hints:

▲ Answer all questions, and answer honestly. Even if the answer is "I don't know" or "Let me think about it," remember that this is a time when children are checking to see if you can provide real help and knowledge.

▲ If you're unclear about your child's question or statement, restate it. For example, you might say, "Are you telling me that—?"

▲ Do allow your child some privacy. This is a time when children begin to write in secret diaries, post "no trespassing" signs on their doors, and hold whispered conversations with friends for hours. A need for privacy is not a sign of out-of-bounds behavior. (This does not apply, however, to reasonable parental safeguards for inappropriate Internet communication, television, and talking on the phone.)

▲ Don't make promises you cannot keep. It's okay to be hopeful and optimistic; just remember that this is an important time of building

3

school years has been left behind, and the independence-seeking tension of the teen years has not begun.

Write on a chalkboard or newsprint the parents' goal for these years:
to help your child
▲ explore his or her world
▲ make good choices
▲ feel competent and successful.

Ask:

Why is communication important now?
Summarize the material in each of the three sections:
▲ Build the habit.
▲ Reason and negotiate.
▲ Be available to listen and process.

How to Improve Communication

(8-10 minutes)
Consider these three main issues carefully. Allow time for discussion and sharing of ideas. (Note: With school violence increasing, security may be the most difficult area to address. There will be further help on this issue in the session on *Your Child and Violence.*)

Quickly review the "other helpful hints" and "Activities to Try."

Conversation Alternatives

(2-3 minutes)
Invite the class to offer other ideas besides the two mentioned here. What works best for them?

trust. Try to be realistic in your plans.

▲ Don't be surprised to hear "I hate you" and other angry comments. Children this age are learning how to express frustration, fear, and anger, yet their vocabulary is still limited. Encourage your child to rail at the boundaries rather than at you.

Activities to Try

▲ Take time to talk about the details of your child's day. Your child may tell rambling stories, but he or she needs your time and attention.

▲ Develop a "secret sign" that the two of you can share silently whenever you want to say "I need to talk to you."

▲ Try family meetings. Every family needs to have a forum where the child can see that what he or she brings to the family is important. This is especially important if there are younger or older siblings. Take time to appreciate and recognize together what each child does well.

▲ Teach your child that displaying a broad range of emotions is good. Name an increasingly diverse and specific number of emotions. Allow your child to discuss daily what made him or her happy, sad, mad, scared, and so forth.

▲ Let a younger child tell you his or her thoughts by drawing pictures. Help the child describe emotions through colors or shapes. Talk about what the child's picture means.

Conversation Alternatives

Sometimes you just need to be in the right place at the right time. Spontaneous or nonstructured situations can be some of the most effective ways to improve communication with your child. Here are a couple of ideas for starters:

▲ Be the driver. When possible, provide transportation for your child and his or her friends to activities and events. You may learn a great deal more about their interests and concerns from their energetic conversations in the backseat than you would from a direct question.

▲ Eat together as a family. Family mealtime is an important way to build identity as a team; it's also a great "training ground" for group conversation. Make this time when family members are able to talk about their day, share stories, and enjoy being together. You'll find that family meals will become a time to "check in"

4

with one another, helping you to become aware of your child's fears and concerns.

Communication Stoppers

▲ Blaming or accusing. Be as clear as possible about desired behavior changes or concerns you may have without being negative about your child and his or her personality and overall ability. Using insulting language may tell your child that you have low expectations and that he or she should not try to improve.

▲ Being dismissive. Your body language and expressions tell your child if you're really listening.

▲ Teasing or not taking your child seriously. Be sensitive to little issues that may be very important to your child.

▲ Being overly critical or having unreasonable expectations. Keep in mind the age of your child.

Two Important Developmental Characteristics

1. Aggressive emotions. During the elementary years, children begin to deal more with emotions that can trigger aggressive behavior, such as jealousy and anger—particularly in peer relationships. Talk with your child about his or her feelings, and help your child channel these feelings in productive ways. For example, if your daughter comes home from school and is furious with Tommy, a boy in her class who made fun of her, ask questions about what happened and how she feels, such as "Why are you angry?" and "Did he hurt your feelings?" Let her know that you understand why she is angry and that it is all right. Focus on how she can take care of herself. Questions to ask might include "Do you need to tell Tommy how you felt?" and "Do you need to avoid him at play time?" When the problem seems to warrant intervention, talk with your child's teacher and/or school guidance counselor.

2. Sassy behavior. Expect a little more assertive behavior as your child approaches the fifth or sixth grade. As your child prepares for the independence of adolescence, he or she may begin to question you more and/or ask for explanations in a new way. Notice the difference between those times when your child is speaking his or her mind and those times when your child is showing actual dis-

5

Communication Stoppers
(4-5 minutes)
Remind the class that even though Conversation Stoppers change somewhat with the age of your child, the basic tenet is to treat your child with the same respect you would afford a friend.

Developmental Characteristics
(5-6 minutes)
Emotions
Dealing with emotions is hard even for some adults. Reassure parents that feelings are not right or wrong; they just are. The parent's role is to help the child

▲ identify the emotion
▲ express it appropriately
▲ develop skills to cope with the situation

Sassy behavior
Remind parents of the Gathering Time exercise: "A parent's job is work himself out of a job."

Say:
Your goal is to raise a son or daughter who can think for himself and make good decisions on his own. As much as you want to do that, it may be uncomfortable when you begin to see the child developing opin-

ions that are different from yours. Remember that disagreeing is not necessarily disrespectful. Parents: A word of warning from the trenches--some children are precocious:
the "teen years" may begin at 10 instead of 13.

When to Seek Help
(4-5 minutes)

Review the warning signs that a child may need professional help in coping. Remind parents that children as well as teenagers may suffer from depression or other problems. If a child had a physical illness, they would seek help. They should not hesitate to do so if the problem is of a mental or social nature.

Your Assignment
(1-2 minutes)

Invite parents to keep a journal during the coming week of conversations they have with their child--real conversations about something the child is interested in, not the usual parental litany of "clean up your room, do your homework, take out the trash." Keep a record of who initiated the conversation, how much time was involved, where the conversation took place, who else was present.

respect. Keep in mind that it is not really disrespectful for a child to ask, "Why do I have to do this?"

When to Seek Help
Remember that children go through many changes, particularly in the upper elementary grades. However, if you find communication with your child difficult and nothing you try seems to work, you may want to seek additional help. Some "warning signs" include the following:

▲ Your child has regular, uncontrollable emotional outbursts or mood swings.
▲ Your child has threatened to harm self or others. (Verbal threats can be deadly warnings. Let your child know that you will assume he or she is serious about any threat.)
▲ Your child's actions or words regularly interfere with social, academic, or family development.
▲ Your child's behaviors are continually disruptive to the family.
▲ Your child avoids school, or has frequent headaches or stomachaches that keep him or her from school. (Look for triggers that may be causing this reaction.)

In the elementary years, children are generally happy and energetic. If your child seems consistently dejected or sad, there may be a problem. Listen for frequent disparaging remarks, such as "They'd never choose me," or "I never get it right." Such comments may indicate a problem with social development.

For girls, fourth through sixth grade is a time when eating disorders often emerge. Although you may not see any behavior changes at this time, listen for concerns about dieting or working out. In these grades, girls are often bigger or taller than boys and may be going through a period of weight gain.

Older elementary boys sometimes exhibit violent or uncooperative behavior. Such behavior could be related to a child's self-image problems or to problems he or she is having in school.

For both boys and girls, if there is a sudden change in school performance, a pattern of school avoidance, or a sudden development of behavior problems, you may want to check for learning disabilities, dyslexia, or vision problems.

Sources for Help
Your first and best source for help and information will be your child's elementary school teacher.

6

This professional sees your child every day as he or she interacts with other children in class and on the playground. Your child's teacher also sees your child's reaction to challenges in school and observes his or her development in comparison to a classroom of children of similar age.

Another excellent source for help is a Christian counselor or family therapist. Your church may have an association with a counselor or may be able to offer recommendations. You also can check with the American Association of Marriage and Family Therapists. They have an on-line directory of licensed therapists by city and state at www.aamft.org.

The Faith Perspective
1 Samuel 1:27-28

"For this child I prayed; and the Lord has granted me the petition that I made to him. Therefore I have lent him to the Lord; as long as he lives, he is given to the Lord." (NRSV)

In a few short years children move from full reliance on their parents to increasing competence.

The child who recently needed help in pouring a glass of juice now can hand out sandwiches in a soup kitchen. The child who beamed when first scrawling the letters of his or her name, can now sound out the words of scripture.

Throughout the Bible we see how the young were used and valued by God: Miriam hid her brother Moses in the bulrushes and reunited their family, Samuel served in the temple, and David faced the giant enemy Goliath. God has given us our children to nurture for a few fleeting years. Our responsibility is to pray for and with them as they grow and face new challenges and to "lend" them to God. Children are eager to put their energies and budding skills to work for God's purposes. These young disciples are ready to find their places in the family of faith.

Look at this month's calendar. Does it reflect your commitment to help your children become grounded people of faith? Block out some time for church and Sunday School and other faith-building and service activities. Why not draw a cross into every daily square when you pray for your child. Your prayers prepare the holy ground they will travel in their own lives of faith.

7

Parents may be surprised by the patterns they discover.

Read:
1 Samuel 1:27-28
During the elementary years, we see our children grow from dependent youngsters to competent young people. Pray for them daily as they learn, fail, try, and grow.

Closing
(1-2 minutes)
Close with this prayer or one of your own:
O Lord, You hear our prayers with such love and care. Help us to listen to our children with that same careful love, and may our words to them be grace-filled. In Jesus' name. Amen.

Library of Help Resources

For parents or classes who want to explore this topic more deeply, review the library of resources offered at www.FaithHome.com. Books are grouped by topic and include general and faith selections.

Recommended Resources

Books That Build Character: A Guide to Teaching Your Child Moral Values Through Stories, by William Kilpatrick and Gregory and Suzanne M. Wolfe (Simon & Schuster, 1994).

My Faith Journal, by Karen Hill (Thomas Nelson, 1997).

Taking Charge of ADHD: The Complete, Authoritative Guide for Parents, by Russell A. Barkley (Guilford Press, 2000).

10 Most Common Mistakes Good Parents Make: And How to Avoid Them, by Kevin Steede, Ph.D. (Prima Publishing, 1998).

For more resources visit www.FaithHome.com.

About the Authors

D. Tony Rankin parents with his wife, Amber. They have three children: Drew, Caleb, and Katelin. When he's not parenting, coaching baseball, or dancing with his daughter at her recitals, he is the director and clinical therapist of The Counseling Center in Nashville, Tennessee. In addition to numerous advice columns and magazine articles, he is the author of *When True Love Doesn't Wait*. He enjoys speaking at seminars and conventions and has taught as an adjunct instructor in psychology and religion at Belmont University .

Cynthia Ezell is a licensed marriage and family therapist in private practice in Nashville, Tennessee. She is also a certified Imago Relationship therapist and a certified group psychotherapist. She is the author of "Growing Up," a monthly column on parenting appearing in *Nashville Parent* magazine. She is the proud mother of three daughters.

FaithHome for Parents provides the church community with resources to support families and help children *to increase their faith, confirm their hope, and perfect them in love.*

ISBN 068708887-9

Communicating with Your Teenager

Learn the Art of Truly Talking with Your Child

FaithHome for Parents™

Gathering Time
(4 minutes)
Have available paper and pens or pencils. Write this question on a chalkboard or newsprint: What is your long-range goal for your teenage son or daughter?

As class members arrive, invite them to give this some serious consideration and write down a one sentence answer.
(Couples in the class may want to work together on this.)

Prayer
When the group has gathered and most have finished writing their goals, pray this prayer or one of your own:
Dear Lord, We thank you for the gift of our teenagers. They are both fascinating and exasperating, some days the hope of the future, yet on others, they seem completely hopeless. We pray for grace and wisdom to guide them through turbulent waters and launch them into faithful, useful lives, for Jesus' sake. Amen.

Scenario

(4 minutes)

Read the scene described at the beginning of the booklet.

Discuss the following question in light of the booklet's next paragraph ("The developmental task..."):

Ask:

What is the hardest part of parenting a teen? What is the hardest part of being a teen?

Why Is Communication Important?

(3 minutes)

Ask:

What does your teen most need from you during this time of change?

Scripture

Read Proverbs 6:20-22 from page 7 in the booklet.

Say:

Even when you think your teen is not listening to anything you say, your words are being "stored in memory," just like a computer. Your words will influence your teen's actions and beliefs for the rest of his life.

"Leave me alone, and stay out of my business!" is the only reply thirteen-year-old Josh gives his father after coming home from an afternoon party. Josh's dad remembers just a couple of years ago when he and his son talked almost every day. What happened?

The developmental task or job of all teenagers is to move away from dependence on us, their parents, and become more independent. Frustration arises when their great need for independence conflicts with a very real continuing dependence on us for food, shelter, transportation, and support. As they recognize their dependence on us, they may direct their frustration as anger toward us, their parents, rather than toward circumstances or rules.

Why Is Communication So Important During the Teen Years?

Your teenage child needs to establish himself as a unique and different person from you. He may be defining and creating differences daily between his new identity and you, his parent. Your teen needs you to be steady and consistent while he experiments with who he is. Be aware that your teen's experimentation in interests, beliefs, style, and expression does not necessarily mean that she is abandoning the family's value system. Rather, she is questioning and reaffirming this value system for herself.

Proverbs 22:6 reads: "Train children in the right way, and when old, they will not stray" (NRSV). Many of us forget the phrase "when old." The teen years are a time of experimentation. It is important to keep conversation and support available as your teen does some experimenting within the safety of the family and household.

Changes to Anticipate with Your Teen

Although all teenagers do not mature at the same rate, the following descriptions and tips may help you to understand and handle the sequence of changes that occur in most teens.

12–13-Year-Olds

Around this time, teens experience anxiety about physical changes, including changes in height, voice, complexion, sexual development, and body shape. Girls may be gaining a little weight and becoming taller than some boys in their class. Boys may be eating a great deal and developing stronger body odor. These physical changes often result in feelings of awkwardness and self-consciousness.

2

Communication tip: This is a time to be particularly sensitive and encouraging to your teen about his or her appearance and new ventures. It's very important not to tease your child about these changes—even in good-natured joking. He or she gets enough of that at school. You are a mirror for your child and his or her self-perception. This is an important time when fathers can help their daughters establish good self-esteem related to their appearance and growth toward sexual maturity. Compliment your daughter on her appearance. Give her hugs and reassurance.

14–15-Year-Olds

Often these teens display their development issues through moodiness and conflicts with friends. For girls, this struggle may show up in daily arguments with their mothers about clothes, curfews, friends, and makeup. Boys in this age group often detach, spending a lot more time alone in their rooms or out with their friends.

Communication tip: Talk with your teen about emotions. Listen to your teen's stories of the everyday social dramas with friends. Ask your teen to describe what makes him or her angry or frustrated.

16–18-Year-Olds

As they approach high school graduation, teens desire even more independence. As a result, they may appear to be disinterested in former interests, or they may express a need to make their own choices in school or church. Learn to trust your teen and be flexible within parameters. Teens in this stage may feel "invincible" and may not understand your concerns about safety.

Communication tip: Letting your child experiment with freedom and learn from some "safe mistakes" will help prepare him or her for the first year away from home. Explain your values and your feelings, establish boundaries, and stick to them. Be willing to listen to your teen's frustrations.

Hints for Improving Communication with Your Teen

▲ Take some time to think about your own teen years and your relationship with your parents during that time. Areas that were important to you as a teen—whether areas of success or failure—may be particularly important to you now as hopes for your child. Be aware of these areas, and keep in

Changes to Anticipate

(5-6 minutes)

As you highlight the "what-to-expect-at-this-age" segments, don't miss the tips for better communication with each age.

▲ 12-13 years: encourage their efforts and compliment their appearance

▲ 14-15 years: talk about emotions

▲ 16-18 years: experiment with independence

Hints for Improving Communication

(8-10 minutes)

Some of these ideas may be obvious to experienced parents, while to others they may be completely new. Take time to discuss each one sufficiently for everyone to "get it." Because it is so important, encourage parents to spend 2-3 minutes in silent reflection on the first one: "Take time to think…"

The sixth one ("Learn to communicate through disagreements…") may be a good one to illustrate with a role play. Invite two class members to act out the discussion between a parent and a teen who wants to go to an unsupervised party.

3

Use the four steps under this tip.

Key Point Summary

▲ Think about your own teen years and interests

▲ Be present for the opportunities

▲ Be honest—especially when you don't know

▲ Anger isn't personal

▲ Apologize

▲ Communicate through disagreements
  Listen
  Mirror
  Empathize
  Give options

▲ Maintain self respect

▲ No power struggles

▲ 24 hour no questions asked rule

▲ Find time

▲ Be around

▲ Try challenges together

mind that your child may not be as concerned about them as you are. For example, if you were an athlete in high school, you may be overly concerned about the athletic performance of your child. Ask yourself: "Is my teen interested and concerned about athletics, or does he or she have other, more intense interests?"

▲ Be present. You may have to take the moments when they come—and often they come late at night. Try to be there when your teen comes home from a date, ball game, or party. Being available when your teen is excited and has a lot to "process" is a good time for communication.

▲ Address all questions honestly, even if the answer is "I don't know" or "I can't answer that now." As your child matures, the questions become harder. Be aware of times when your answer may need to be that you, as a parent, need time to think or find more information.

▲ Depersonalize your teen's anger. Remember that this anger isn't really directed at you. Help your teen target circumstances, rules, and boundaries as the source of his or her emotions.

▲ Apologize when appropriate. It's good to say you're sorry when you've spoken too quickly or harshly, or when you've made a mistake.

▲ Learn to communicate through disagreements with your teen. Here are some steps to try:
  ✔ Listen to and validate your teen's feelings. (I understand that you are angry.)
  ✔ Mirror or restate those feelings to make sure you understand. (It makes sense that you would like to go to this party.)
  ✔ Empathize. (I would be frustrated, too, if my parents wouldn't allow me to go to a party that was important to me.)
  ✔ State options clearly and specifically. (As your parent, it is my job to care for your safety, and I am not comfortable with you going to parties where there will be no adult supervision.)

▲ Maintain respect for yourself as a parent and a person. Acknowledge that your needs and those of the family are important too. Let your child know of these concerns. For example, you might say, "I am willing to work with you, but I have concerns about—."

▲ Don't get involved in power struggles. Once you have made your decision, be available to listen to concerns; but do not argue about the rightness

4

of the rule or the responses from other kids and parents. Your child has a right to have feelings of frustration. You have the responsibility of setting safe, secure boundaries.

▲ Try the "24-hour no questions asked" rule. All teens sometimes get into situations where they need help but may not feel comfortable enough to call Mom or Dad. To make certain that you are there to keep your child safe, offer to pick up your teen and his or her friends "anytime, anywhere" when they need help. The "no questions asked" simply means that each of you will have time to go home and sleep before talking.

▲ Give your teen your time. The best thing you can do to foster good two-way communication with your child is to allow time to be together. Whether it's a long walk or a burger out together, try to find time each week to spend one-on-one with your teen.

▲ Put yourself where your child is. Be the house where kids gather. You'll learn more about your teen if your house is a gathering spot. You'll also know your teen's friends better.

▲ Try hard things together. During the teen years, your child will be trying many challenging things for the first time. Share your own challenges with your teen, telling about some of the hard things you may be facing in your life or career. Celebrate each other's efforts and risk-taking as much as your successes.

Communication Stoppers

▲ Defensiveness ("It's not my fault that—.")
▲ Stonewalling ("I'm just not going to talk about this—.")
▲ Exaggeration ("You always do this—. You never do that—.")

Safeguards to Consider

▲ Set house rules. While kids are becoming more independent, spending time in private places without supervision—such as your empty house—can be very dangerous. Therapists who work with teens report that the hours of 3:00 to 6:00 P.M. are the most prevalent hours for beginning experimentation with alcohol, drugs, and sex. If your child is at home alone during these hours, set boundaries about who can be in the house. And don't just call to check on things; drop in occasionally. Rules and enforce-

5

Communication Stoppers
(4-5 minutes)
Review these quickly--they change with the age of the child!

Communication Starters
Divide the class into groups of three or four. Ask each group to think of two questions that they could use to start a meaningful conversation with their teen. Write their responses on a board or newsprint. Some possiblities:

▲ "What do you think about (name a topic or issue)?
▲ "What do you want to be doing in five years?"
▲ What is your favorite movie? (band, team) Why?
▲ What do you worry about?

Safeguards
(7-8 minutes)
This section is about boundary setting and boundary keeping. It is an important way to let a teenager know how important he is to you: "Do you care enough to make sure I am where I am supposed to be?"

Parents are a great resource for each other. The simple knowledge that parents talk to each other is sometimes enough to keep a teenager honest!

When to Seek Help

(5-6 minutes)
One of the goals of a teen is to separate himself, to be different from his parents--sometimes to the parents' horror. Use this section to reassure parents that most teen fads disappear as quickly as they came. However, encourage parents to take seriously the "more dramatic changes" listed. Ask your pastor for the name of a counselor or therapist in your town, and have that information available for your class.

ment will help your teen make good decisions. Remember, often it is difficult for them to stand up to peers alone.

▲ Build a parent network. Being informed and involved is invaluable. Know the parents of your teen's friends; call and check in with one another frequently. This also will be a great support network for each of you.

When to Seek Help

As teenagers grow to independence, most want to exercise their own choices in music, clothing, friends, and social activities. Some of the changes are unsettling to parents yet are not, on their own, danger signs. Many healthy teens may

▲ radically change their clothing style—wearing all black, dramatic makeup, or odd jewelry;
▲ experiment with hair color, tattoos, or extra earrings;
▲ become interested in new and different hobbies;
▲ feel less or different interest in church activities;
▲ change friends;
▲ experiment with grim or startling poetry or music.

Most of these choices, alone, are quite normal. To help you deal with these kinds of changes and your own feelings about them, gather a group of parents who have teens around the age of your child. Talking together and sharing advice, support, and ideas may help. Be flexible and allow your child to experiment with safe issues such as clothing and hobbies. Ask sincere questions about why he or she is trying something new.

You may want to seek help from a Christian counselor or family therapist if your teen demonstrates more dramatic changes, such as:

▲ withdrawing from all friends;
▲ becoming disinterested in all school and church activities;
▲ refusing to eat or exhibiting dramatic weight loss;
▲ having very extreme mood swings;
▲ making specific threats about suicide or hurting himself/herself;
▲ threatening harm to you or other family members.

Remember that when teens try a lot of new and different things, they are sharpening their identity and looking for a place to fit in. It is normal for them to be excited about something—even if it is just hanging out with friends. If your teen drops interest in everything, this may be a sign of depression.

If you need to consult with a counselor or theraist, check with your church for referrals to a Christian counselor, or try the online directory of licensed family therapists through The American Association of Marriage and Family Therapists. You can find names and numbers of therapists in your area by accessing their website at www.aamft.org.

What If "the Worst" Happens?

What if you receive a phone call late at night, asking you to come to the station and pick up your child? First, know that this does not mean that you are a failed parent. Many families, probably within your own church community, have been there too.

▲ Meet your child with compassion. The toughest thing for him or her might be facing you when you arrive.

▲ Deal with the legal problem first, setting aside the questions for a later time.

▲ Be the advocate for your child. Support your teen while respecting and upholding the legal consequences imposed.

▲ Seek help. Call a friend with legal experience. Your pastor may have a suggestion.

▲ Talk with your teen about why the behavior occurred. What drove the action—need for attention from peers or from you? need for acceptance? an addiction that needs attention?

You may want to consider family therapy, a type of therapy where parent(s) and child meet together with a counselor. This sends a message to your child that you're in it together, rather than reaffirming your child's feeling that he or she is "the problem." For help or suggestions with drug or alcohol problems, call your local Crisis Line, which should have lists of a variety of programs that can offer help.

Know that life goes on. Many successful adults and their parents have been through a tumultuous youth. Ask your pastor or friends at church for suggestions of parents of children who have gone through similar experiences and can be mentors for you.

The Faith Perspective
Proverbs 6:20-22

My child, keep your father's commandment,
  and do not forsake your mother's teachings.
Bind them upon your heart always;
  tie them around your neck.
When you walk, they will lead you;
  when you lie down, they will watch over you;
  and when you awake, they will talk with you. (NRSV)

7

What If "the Worst" Happens
(8-9 minutes)

No one expects the unexpected. Carefully prepare parents to imagine themselves in this position. Some of your class members may have experienced such an event and may (or may not!) volunteer their own insights. Be sure to respect a teen's and a family's privacy.

Family therapy, suggested in this section, is valuable when a teen is involved in risky or seriously rebellious behaviors. Remind your class that teens are products of, and inhabitants of, a family unit. The teen may be the "canary in the coal mine," indicating that there is a problem with family dynamics.

Closing

(1 minute)

Invite the class to practice really listening to their teenagers this week.

Close with this prayer or one of your own:

O God of all humankind, we know that sometimes You must feel exactly as we do: that You have created these persons who are so difficult and stubborn, who think they know best, who don't want to listen to what You can teach them. As we live each day with our sons and daughters, Help us to remember the love, the grace and patience You have extended to Your children, that we may do the same to ours, in the name of Christ. Amen.

Years spent loving and teaching your teen provide a thin but strong shield of wisdom they can use in life. When it seems they aren't listening, they are. When it seems they don't care, they do. When it seems they don't believe, they are struggling to figure out what to believe. When they ignore your instructions, they are trying on life without your protection. They will learn. Show up for your teen today. Your constant presence will help foster their understanding of the God who never forsakes them.

Recommended Resources

Positive Parenting Your Teens: The A to Z Book of Sound Advice, and Practical Solutions, by Karen Renshaw Joslin and Mary Bunting Decher (Fawcett Books, 1997).

This Too Shall Pass, by Kel Groseclose (Dimensions for Living, 1995).

365 Meditations for Mothers of Teens (Dimensions for Living, Nashville, 1996).

For more resources visit www.FaithHome.com.

About the Authors

D. Tony Rankin parents with his wife, Amber. They have three children: Drew, Caleb, and Katelin. When he's not parenting, coaching baseball, or dancing with his daughter at her recitals, he is the director and clinical therapist of The Counseling Center in Nashville, Tennessee. In addition to numerous advice columns and magazine articles, he is the author of *When True Love Doesn't Wait.* He enjoys speaking at seminars and conventions and has taught as an adjunct in psychology and religion instructor at Belmont University.

Cynthia Ezell is a licensed marriage and family therapist in private practice in Nashville, Tennessee. She is also a certified Imago Relationship therapist and a certified group psychotherapist. She is the author of "Growing Up," a monthly column on parenting appearing in *Nashville Parent* magazine. She is the proud mother of three daughters.

FaithHome for Parents provides the church community with resources to support families and help children *to increase their faith, confirm their hope, and perfect them in love.*

Copyright © 1999 by Abingdon Press.
All rights reserved.
1-800-672-1789

ISBN 068708888-7

Teaching Your Child to Pray

Learning the Basics
of Prayer for Children

FaithHome
for Parents™

Gathering Time
(5-8 minutes)

Post a sign on or near the door "Please enter quietly in a spirit of prayer." Hand each person a note as they enter, asking them begin this session praying silently for their children by name. Suggest they give thanks for the child, offer petitions for the child's physical and spiritual growth, ask forgiveness for their failings as a parent, and for guidance in raising that child.

Prayer
(6-8 minutes)

When everyone has arrived and had time for their prayers, open with this prayer or one of your own:
O Holy One,
Teach us to pray,
Hold us close to You, and
Touch us with Your power.
And now, speak to our hearts
in this silence, Lord....
(Pause....)
Amen.

Scenario

Read the scenario from the booklet (the story printed in italics).

Ask:

Do you have memories of childhood bedtime prayers? Is that a custom you are passing on to your children?

▲ Why are bedtime prayers important for children?

▲ What did Lauren's father learn about her as he listened to her prayers?

Invite the class to consider the influence a parent has on the child's prayer life. The pattern that is learned as a child is frequently continued into the next generation.

Say:

I'm not going to ask how many of you sit with your children while they say their prayers. It might be embarrassing for some. But think about whether you are following the same pattern your parents set. Are you doing (or not doing) the same thing your parents did? Do you see the importance of this? It can influence generations! What you are doing is most probably what your children will do with their children.

Lauren climbed into bed, and her father tucked her in. As he sat down on the edge of the bed, he said, "Are you ready to say a prayer?"

"Dear God," Lauren began, "thank you for Mommy and Daddy and Bethany. Thank you for all good things. Help Grandma get well, and help me feel better about school. Watch over everyone tonight. Amen."

He kissed her goodnight and turned out the light. As he took one last look at his daughter nestled snugly in her bed, he smiled, remembering a time nearly thirty years earlier when his mother had sat on his bed while he prayed.

I remember that night as if it were yesterday, and I remember just as vividly my own childhood ritual of bedtime prayer. Every night my mother and I would talk about the activities of the day before saying a bedtime prayer. My childhood prayers were much the same as the prayer spoken by my daughter Lauren: both included the significant people in our lives. As a father, I have learned what my mother also learned as she sat on my bed listening to her child pray: our children's thoughts and the yearnings of their hearts are expressed in their prayers. As I listened to my daughter's prayer that night, I heard the concerns that she had carried through the day. Her prayer gave me a glimpse of her needs and her trust that God was with her as her friend.

Prayer is a language of the heart. Whether the language is spoken or remains silent, prayer gives us a tool to express our inner thoughts and emotions. Prayer also provides a means for us to support others, even those persons we have never met. Prayer is our special connection with God.

Prayer is an ongoing conversation and growing friendship with God through words and thoughts. When we pray with our children, we are sharing the relationship we have

2

with God at the same time that we are expressing our love for our children.

How Can I Teach My Child to Pray?
1. Begin where the child is.

It is never too early or too late to teach your child to pray. With an infant, you can begin by singing "Jesus Loves Me" and speaking simple words of thanks for your child—such as, "Thank you, God, for Kyle"—during "cuddling time." With an older child, pause at mealtime and bedtime to say a few words of thanks for the meal and the day.

Prayers of thanks are a good way to teach children to pray; even very young children can name things for which they are thankful. Be sure to use your child's name in your own prayers of thanks. This will teach your child that she or he is important to God. Remember that your child can begin to experience a relationship with God without having to understand that relationship. As a parent, you want your child to know that God is personal. God is ready to hear the words of even the youngest child, because God is present with each of us.

2. Establish a regular pattern of prayer.

A friend told me that his family gathered for prayer every morning before the children went out the door to meet the school bus. The children looked forward to holding hands in their family circle as the day began. They knew that whatever they faced during the day, God would be with them.

Children learn through ritual and routine. Mealtime and bedtime are two good occasions for establishing a ritual.

Saying a prayer before a meal reminds a child that we are part of the world God has made, and that we are grateful for the food we need in order to live. You may want to use the same prayer before each meal, find

3

How Can I Teach My Child to Pray?
(10 minutes)

1. Begin where the child is. Keep prayers simple; children can understand "just talking to God." Conversational prayers are great for kids, because they can just say what is on their minds, instead of worrying about saying it "right." Tell your child that God loves him and wants to hear from him. Talk about how all of us like to hear from people we love: grandparents, aunts and uncles, friends. That's how we maintain relationships.

2. Establish a regular pattern of prayer. Ask class members to share their rituals and routines of prayer. Do they pray regularly? When? Who actually says the prayer?

One of the advantages of mealtime and bedtime prayers is their regularity. They are everyday activities. Also, both give a child an opportunity to pray for others: at meals, we pray for those less fortunate, and at bedtime, we commit those we love into God's keeping.
Bedtime is sometimes anxi-

ety-ridden for children. Sleep may be associated with separation, darkness, and oblivion, like a mini-death. The parent's presence in quieting the child and saying the prayers is a powerful reminder of God's love and care through the night.

3. Help your child to memorize some simple prayers. Many parents rely on "God is great, God is good..." and "Now I lay me down to sleep...." There are other prayers available as well. Look in your hymnal for prayers to be said or for prayer hymns or choruses. Check your Church Library, too. Children memorize easily so don't be afraid to start.

4. Model prayer for your child. Take turns saying grace at the table. Allow your children to hear you pray for them. Let them hear you talk about prayer as part of decision-making ("I'll have to pray about that.")

several prayers from which to choose, or create a new prayer each time. Hold hands around the table or fold your hands as the prayer is said by one or by all.

Bedtime has always been our family's time to quiet ourselves and prayerfully reflect on the day that is past. Now that our children are teenagers, they still expect a visit from Mom or Dad before they go to sleep. As you help your child get ready for bed, let this be a time to give thanks and pray for each other.

Look for other times and ways to make prayer a regular part of your family's life together. Your child will begin to anticipate your special prayer rituals and may even remind you when it's time to pray!

3. Help your child to memorize some simple prayers.

Teaching children some simple prayers they can recite from memory helps ease them into the practice of prayer. Be sure to say the prayers aloud with your child to help him or her feel relaxed and confident. Work on learning one prayer, repeating it for several days or weeks until your child has memorized it. Then begin working on another prayer. Start simple and work up to longer, more difficult prayers as your child grows and/or is ready. There are many wonderful collections of children's prayers from which to choose, including some beautifully illustrated books that you can enjoy together (see the list of Recommended Resources).

When your child is ready for more difficult prayers, be sure to include the Lord's Prayer. Jesus offered this prayer as an example of how we are to pray (see Luke 11:1-4). It contains specific guidelines for prayer: praise, thanks, forgiveness, and direction. Children do not need to fully understand the words in order to memorize

4

the prayer. In fact, even four- and five-year-olds have been known to master the prayer in a relatively short time. Teaching your child the Lord's Prayer at home—rather than waiting for your child to learn it at church—will help to make an important "link" between home and church.

4. Model prayer for your child.

Children learn the importance of prayer by watching and listening as their parents pray.

At a recent gathering of our extended family, one of the children was asked to say the mealtime prayer. Everyone listened intently to the words of the child. Later it occurred to me that the children usually were asked to say the mealtime prayer at these gatherings but rarely were given the opportunity to hear an adult pray.

We adults look forward to hearing children pray, but it is important for children to know that prayer isn't just for kids. Pray daily for your child. Pray daily with your child. Allow your child to see the importance of prayer in your own life.

What Should I Teach My Child About Prayer?

1. Prayer is simply talking with God.

Children need to know that they can talk to God just as they would talk to a parent or a good friend—wherever and whenever they want. God is always ready to listen.

One day I was driving with our two children in the car. Suddenly an ambulance approached from behind us. I pulled the car to the side of the road and said aloud, "God, take care of those who are hurt." By responding to the situation with a simple prayer, I demonstrated my belief that God is with us wherever we are and cares about what is happening to us.

Look for opportunities to offer simple, spontaneous prayers in the presence of your

5

What Should I Teach My Child About Prayer?

(20 minutes)

Before they teach their children about prayer, parents should give some thought to what they themselves believe. Divide the class into groups of three or more and briefly discuss these questions:

▲ Are there things that are too small or unimportant to take to God in prayer?

▲ Do you take time to listen to God?

▲ Do you ever just tell God how you feel?

▲ How do you experience answers to prayer?

Parents may learn some things about prayer from this session too!

Write these headings on a chalkboard or newsprint as you discuss them:
1. Prayer is talking wih God.
2. Prayer involves listening.
3. God answers prayer.

Closing

(4-5 minutes)

Your Assignment

If you are not already doing regular prayers with your children, begin this week. Have a family council to talk with everyone about this new aspect of your family life and why you want to do it. You may want to start with a prayer at the dinner table, then later on, add bedtime prayers.

Read Romans 8:38-39. The Good News is that nothing can separate us from God. Nothing can keep us away from God. God is always with us.

Close with this prayer or one of your own:
Eternal God, we come before You amazed by Your love and concern for us. Thank You for hearing and answering our prayers. Help us to take the time to listen for Your word for us, and may we always find joy in Your Presence. Amen.

child—such as thanking God for a beautiful sunset, expressing your concern for a sick friend or pet, or asking for God's help with a particular problem or situation. Remember that the best way to teach your child to pray is by your own example.

2. Prayer involves listening as well as speaking.

In his book *Bringing up Children in the Christian Faith*, John Westerhoff writes that "prayer is what God does to us rather than anything we do to God" (Minneapolis, Minn.: Winston Press, 1980, p. 45). Listening is as important to prayer as speaking. The psalmist writes, "Be still and know that I am God" (Psalm 46:10). For a conversation to be meaningful, someone must be listening. Prayer is our conversation with God. If our prayers are to be meaningful, then, we must take time to listen to God.

Being quiet and listening do not come naturally for most children. As a child, I tried to follow the long prayers of the Sunday worship service, but usually my mind would wander and I would think about the people and things important to me. Yet because of what I had learned about prayer, I knew that God was with me when I prayed. I knew that prayer was my special time alone with God. I believed it was the time when God was thinking about me.

How can you begin to teach your child that prayer involves listening as well as talking? Here are a few ideas you might try:

First of all, find ways to introduce the concept of listening and help your child practice listening, such as spending quiet time together in a rocking chair; listening to quiet, meditative music together; reading to your child; and so forth.

Help your child understand that prayer does not have to be spoken. Ask your child

6

to draw a picture of things for which he or she is thankful or persons he or she loves. Some of the most meaningful "prayers" I have witnessed were drawn by a child.

When praying with your child, ask your child to think quietly about God and the questions he or she has for God.

Take a walk outside and ask your child to listen quietly to all the sounds of God's creation. Then have your child identify as many of those sounds as he or she can. Talk about how we can hear (and see) God in the world around us.

3. God answers prayer, but not always in the ways we want or expect.

As with so many things in life, prayer takes practice. The more we pray, the easier it becomes—and the better we become "hearing God," and at recognizing God's answers to our prayers. God does answer our prayers, but not always how or when we want or expect. Sometimes we pray for healing for someone who does not get better. Sometimes we ask for something that never happens or that we never receive. Explaining this concept to young children can be difficult. The best approach is to keep it simple. Assure your child that although we may not always understand the things that happen and why God chooses to act or not to act in certain ways, we can be sure of God's love for us (*Romans* 8:38-39) and God's promise to be with us always (*Matthew* 28:20*b*).

Prayer takes patience and persistence. In time we learn to listen not for what we want, but for what God wants, trusting that God will always be with us and will help us in ways we may not be able to see or fully understand.

7

Recommended Resources

Children and Prayer: A Shared Journey, by
   Betty Shannon Cloyd, (Upper Room,
   1997).

Prayer Collections

All God's Children: A Book of Prayers, by
   Lee Bennett Hopkins (Harcourt Brace,
   1998).

*I Can Pray with Jesus: The Lord's Prayer for
   Children,* Debbie Trafton O'Neal
   (Augsburg, 1997).

*My Journal; A Place to Write about God and
   Me,* by Janet R. Knight (Upper Room
   Books, 1997).

*Now I Lay Me Down to Sleep: Action Prayers,
   Poems and Songs for Bedtime,* by Debbie
   Trafton O'Neal (Augsburg, 1994).

For more resources visit www.FaithHome.com.

About the Author

   Steve Richards and his wife, Amanda, are
the parents of two teenage daughters. He
serves as pastor to children and their families
at Brentwood United Methodist Church in
Brentwood, Tennessee.

The Scripture quotations contained in this publication are
from the New Revised Standard Version Bible, Copyright ©
1989 by the Division of Christian Education of the National
Council of the Churches of Christ in the United States of
America, and are used by permission. All rights reserved.

**FaithHome for Parents provides the
church community with resources
to support families and help children
*to increase their faith, confirm their hope, and
perfect them in love.***

ISBN 068708906-9

Sharing Faith with Your Child

Making Faith a Part of Everyday Life

FaithHome for Parents™

Gathering Time
(5-8 minutes)

Option 1: If you have time the preceeding week, ask class members to find a picture of someone who represented values of loyalty, faith, honesty or love to them as a child. These might be teachers, grandparents, neighbors or friends. Take a few minutes to share and talk about these important childhood mentors. (Be prepared to get the ball rolling with a photo or two of your own.)

Option 2: Bring a video clip or two or a list of television shows from your childhood that presented parent child relationships (i.e. Andy Griffith, Eddie's Father, The Waltons). From these nostalgic shows, talk about what is timeless and what feels dated. What about the relationships would you like to identify with?

Prayer
(6-8 minutes)

When everyone has arrived, take a moment for silent prayer and thought. Read 1 Corinthians 13: 2-3:

And if I have prophetic powers, and understand all mysteries and all knowledge, and if I have all faith, so as to remove mountains, but do not have love, I am nothing. 3 If I give away all my possessions, and if I hand over my body so that I may boast, but do not have love, I gain nothing. (NRSV)

After a moment, open with this prayer or one of your own:

Gracious God, we thank you for these greatest gifts, our children. As we try everyday to know more, be more, protect more and provide more, help us to remember that the greatest inheritance we can give them is love. Help us show them our love for them and the depths of your great parental love for us all.

Scenario

Read the opening scenario from the booklet (the story printed in italics).

Ask:

▲ What characteristics does Sarah exhibit that you like? (confidence, caring, humor, respect)

▲ What or who causes you the most concern about the story?

▲ Where does "faith" come into the picture?

One day Sarah's mother took her to a public playground, and she immediately began to play with two other little girls. The girls were several years older than five-year-old Sarah, and they were sisters.

As they were playing, the older sister got upset with her younger sister and said to her in anger, "You are stupid and ugly!"

When Sarah heard that, she said, "Word police! Word police!"

The older girl turned to Sarah and asked, "What did you say?"

Sarah repeated, "I said, 'word police.'"

The older girl retorted, "Why did you say that?"

Sarah answered, "I said 'word police' because you said two bad words."

"What bad words did I say?" the older girl questioned.

Sarah responded, "You said 'stupid' and 'ugly,' and those are bad words. And when you say bad words, the 'word police' come out!"

"Oh yeah?" said the older girl. "Well, how about _ _ _ _?" And she blurted out a four-letter word.

Sarah said, "Yep! I think that would be one, too!"

This true-life experience happened to our granddaughter, Sarah, who has a delightful personality and never is at a loss for words. What's interesting about the experience is this: We see that one child is being taught daily how to be loving, gracious, and respectful toward others—and also how to stand tall for what is right and good. She has learned at home and at church that it is not nice to call someone stupid or ugly. In contrast, the other child's parents were sitting right there on a park bench within easy earshot of that colorful conversation. They were reading magazines. They never looked up. They never said a word. They never corrected their daughter.

The Early Years Are So Important

In recent years psychologists have emphasized how important the early years are. Our personalities, attitudes, values, habits, principles, self-esteem, and even I.Q.s are shaped so powerfully by what happens to us in the first few years of life.

I once read a poem that touched my heart called "A Child's Appeal." The poem, written by Mamie

2

ene Cole, uses the first person as if a child is
speaking to the world. The child is essentially saying,
"Here I am, world. You have anticipated my arrival,
and now I'm here—ready to find my special place.
But I need your help. I need your encouragement. I
need your teaching. I need your inspiration. I need
your guidance. My destiny is in your hands." The
poem ends with these powerful words: "Train me, I
beg you, that I may be a blessing to the world."

Just as we begin training our children physically
and mentally when they are very young, so also we
must begin training them spiritually in their earliest
years. There's an old story about a young mother
who asked a noted counselor how soon she should
begin teaching her child the faith. The counselor
asked, "How old is your child?" The mother
answered, "Two." The counselor said, "Hurry
home. You're three years late already." The
counselor was right. It is best to start early. But let
me hurry to say that it's never too late. Starting late
is better than never starting at all. Proverbs 22:6
puts it like this: "Train children in the right way, and
when old, they will not stray" (NRSV).

Where and How Do We Begin?

Most of us know how important it is to share our
faith with our children; the part we struggle with is
knowing where and how to begin. How do we train
our children so that they may be a blessing to the
world? How do we crown their heads with wisdom,
fill their hearts with love, and set them on the right
paths? What are the most important things we can
teach our children?

A fourteen-year-old girl was suspended from
school for cheating. When her mother tried to talk
to her about it, the girl screamed, "So what?
Everything's different now. We don't go by your
rules anymore."

"I guess that's true," the shaken mother said to
me later, "and I don't know how to cope with it."

Well, is that true? Can it be that in this troubled,
stressful, fast-changing world in which we live, the
rules have changed? Have the enduring values
changed so that we're unsure not only of how to
teach our children but also of what to teach them?
Should we just improvise as we go along? Of course
not! No matter how fast times and customs may

3

Where to Begin
(25-30 minutes)

Say:
In the booklet, Jim Moore
tells us that we cannot start
too early in faith training
our children. Like
researchers who play
Mozart to children still in
the womb, we as parents
can start, before their birth,
to consider how we will
help them build faithful
lives - through our family
traditions, the stories we
share, the way we spend
time together and the
examples we set.

Read:
An example in the booklet
involves a young girl
admonishing her parent,
saying "everything is different now." Think back to
some of the nostalgic TV
shows of your own child-
hood (or Nick at Night for
that matter!) What are
some special relationships
you recall?

Ask:
▲ What feels different
about these relationships
& situations compared
to today's "real
life"(neighborhoods,
working moms, school
situations)?
▲ What are some of the
truly basic values you
saw there that you try to

share with your children, even when they are very young. (Answers might include honesty, respect, kindness, generosity, love).

These are all very important in helping to raise our children. We'll focus on three great values: Honesty, Love and Faith.

Teaching children honesty
The author quotes 1 Corinthians 13:6 "(Love) doesn't rejoice in wrongdoing but rejoices in the truth." What does that mean to you?

Honesty is the foundation to good communication, respect, love, self esteem and many other aspects of good family life and society.

Ask:
How can you example and encourage honesty to your children? Some suggestions from the booklet are:
▲ Be honest yourself in everyday situations
▲ Don't "hide" things from others in the family
▲ Never let your child's dishonesty slide

Are there other examples you can think of? What benefits, long term, do you

change, certain values always endure, certain truth always are relevant, certain attitudes always are appropriate, and certain actions always are right. A Christian parents, we have the responsibility of sharing these truths and values—our faith—with o children.

So, where and how do we begin? I couldn't begi to list all the important Christian values and principles we should teach our children, but let me suggest three essential ones.

1. We must teach our children to be honest.
The apostle Paul put it like this: "Love does not rejoice in what is wrong; it rejoices in what is right (1 Corinthians 13:6, *author's paraphrase*). We need to teach our children that integrity is so important. Nothing will ever eliminate the need for honesty. I fact, it is impossible to imagine any decent, desirab society without it. Integrity is the quality of being able to be trusted. It means that we don't lie to on another, that we do what we say we will do, that the affection we profess is genuine, and that the praise we give is honest. Teaching children to live i this way is sometimes difficult because honesty and integrity often seem to be in short supply today.

"I'm so ashamed," a man once said to me. "My teenage son has been helping a friend fix up a second-hand car, and the other day he told us how he had helped sell it, too. He said, 'Hey, Dad, I showed Brian that neat trick with the mileage you used when you got rid of the old Chevy."

We teach our children honesty—or dishonesty—by the way we ourselves live.

A six-year-old boy saw a comic book that he reall wanted, but he only had a nickel. So when the storekeeper was not looking, he took the book. His parents found out and discussed what to do. They agreed the comic book had to be paid for, but they wondered if they could just take the money to the store and explain. After all, he was just a very little boy; and if they talked to him about it, they were certain he would never do it again. Eventually they decided they couldn't treat the situation that lightly So the boy, accompanied by his parents, went back to the store and told the owner what he had done, paid for the book, and asked for forgiveness.

Those parents were right! Honesty and integrity

4

do not come without a price, and although that lesson is best taught when children are young, it is a lesson worth teaching at any age.

Everyday ways to teach honesty:
▲ Be honest in your own dealings with others, such as telling the truth even when it's not convenient or desirable. Children take note when we tell the salesclerk that he has given us back too much change, or when we take a phone call we don't want to take rather than asking a family member to say we're not home.
▲ Don't try to "hide" things from others, especially family members. Trying to hide something can be just as destructive as outright lying about it.
▲ Never allow your children's dishonesty to "slide by." Explain why honesty is so important by discussing relevant scriptures. Determine and discuss reasonable consequences for dishonesty in advance, and be consistent in enforcing them.

2. We must teach our children to love.
The apostle Paul called love "the more excellent way" (1 Cor. 12:31 NRSV) and "the greatest" of all (1 Cor. 13:13 NRSV). We need to give our children love—and lots of it! And we need to show them how to be loving persons.

One day as I was standing in line in a supermarket, I overheard some parents unload a vicious verbal attack on their child. Horrible expletives, dirty names, profane accusations, nasty insinuations, angry put-downs were all aimed directly at a tired little boy who just wanted a five-cent piece of bubble gum. Maybe he didn't need the bubble gum; but even when we say "no," we can say it with respect, can't we? We need to always remember that every child is a child of God, a person of integrity and worth, a person for whom Christ came and died.

One of the ways we teach our children how to be loving persons is by being patient with them, understanding of them, and respectful toward them in every stage of their lives. They will go through stages, and they may go off on tangents; but if we

see in fostering honesty in your own family?

Teaching children to love
Like honesty, we teach our children about love every-day in what we say in the family, our body language, how we spend our time. We can show love to our children and others through showing respect, courtesy patience, and kindness.

Ask:
What are everyday ways you teach and show love with your children? Read the list that the author offers—what other examples can you think of?

What does this have to do with building faith? Some therapists feel that a child's first understanding of a loving and caring God comes from their experience of a loving parent. Your examples of love and caring, even in discipline, build a strong foundation for your child's picture of God.

5

Teaching our children to have faith

Sharing your faith with your child doesn't require a seminary degree, deep theological study or much experience. You're also not in it alone. Providing experiences for your child at church, reading stories together or just talking about what they learned at Vacation Bible school are all great ways to begin.

Say:

Think of your own early influences - were they simple and matter-of-fact or studied? What kinds of experiences do you recall now, looking back? Who had the biggest impact on your first ideas about faith, God and spirituality?

Go over the five everyday ways to teach faith with the class. You may want to write this sum up on a chart or chalkboard.

▲ Talk about God's faitlfulness in your life
▲ Memorize Bible verses
▲ Put God first
▲ Keep promises
▲ Teach trust

The author suggests that faith is as much caught in the family as it is taught. What do you see in the suggestions about teaching

respect our children and they see us treating every person we meet with dignity, respect, kindness, and courtesy, then they will learn how to love. And mos often they will work through the stages and, eventually, come back to the values of their Christia faith, the principles and standards of their home, an the art of love.

The best way to teach children how to be loving persons is to model love—in other words, to teach love not only in our words but also in our actions.

Everyday ways to teach love:
▲ Tell your children how much you love them—then show it.
▲ Live the Golden Rule, especially at home.
▲ Be forgiving and merciful. Never discipline in anger.
▲ Be affectionate! Hug, hold, and kiss your children often.
▲ Always be respectful of your children.

3. We must teach our children to have faith.

Faith is not only what we believe; it is also a way of living. It is a lifestyle. Faith is not a small room stuck on the back of the house; it is the light in all the rooms. In other words, faith is the golden threac that ties all our Christian values and beliefs together. It is the cement that gives us strength and endurance against the storms of life. It's the strong rock upon which we stand. In a word, it is commitment—to God and to what we believe.

Everyday ways to teach faith:
▲ Talk with your children about God's promises and the ways God has been faithful in your own life.
▲ Help your children memorize specific Bible promises or verses of reassurance and recite them together, particularly during difficult or uncertain times.
▲ Demonstrate your commitment to God by putting God first in your life.
▲ Be true to your word. Keep the promises you make, and make promises you plan to keep.
▲ Teach your children to do their best and trust God for the rest.

6

Faith is More "Caught" Than Taught

If you want to teach your children the Christian faith, the best way is to let them see and experience your faith. Of course, you should teach them memorized prayers; but remember it's more important for them to see and hear you pray. Of course, you should encourage them to attend church and Sunday school; but remember it's even more important for them to see you going to church and being excited to be there. You see, the Christian faith is more "caught" than taught. The old saying is so true: What we do speaks more loudly than what we say.

Dr. Dick Murray, one of the leading Christian educators in America today, once said that he had taught his four-year-old grandson, Martin, how to sing "Old MacDonald" and "Row, Row, Row Your Boat"; and he decided that he needed to teach him the "Gloria Patri." So they got in the car, buckled up, and rode through the streets of Dallas singing "Glory Be to the Father..." over and over and over. A short time later, he took Martin to "big church" for the first time; and when they got to that place in the service where the congregation stood together and began to sing the "Gloria Patri," he felt a tug on his coat. He bent down and Martin said excitedly in his ear, "Poppa! They are singing our song!"

Teaching our faith to our children can be as easy and natural as singing or laughing or playing together. Just by watching our example, our children can learn to "sing our song" of faith. Here are some easy ways to make sharing your faith a natural part of everyday life:

▲ Pray daily with your children. In addition to praying before meals, pray spontaneously together at bedtime and other times.
▲ Read the Bible—or Bible stories—together regularly, perhaps at bedtime, before or after a meal, or during a family devotion time.
▲ Eat together as a family as often as possible. Take advantage of opportunities to talk about the ways God is working in your lives.
▲ Include God in everyday conversation, such as saying, "Didn't God paint a beautiful sky today?" or "I was nervous about the sales

7

faith or sharing faith everyday that would work for you?

Faith is Caught

Another way to share faith with your child is to be an example of faith in everyday routine. Refer the group to Dick Murray's story. Do you remember some of your first songs, verses, and stories learned? Review the list of everyday activities.

Your Assignment

Invite the parents in the class to find one or two things in the list that they can accomplish this week. Whether it's as simple as reading a story together, sharing a story about their profession of faith or confirmation or adding a prayer to dinner, ask each parent to commit to adding something to their routine during the next week.

Closing Prayer

Gracious God, we thank you for the community and support of learning together as parents. Help us show your love, patience, kindness and grace in our family this week.

For more study: If your class is interested in more in-depth help about sharing faith with their children, you may be interested in *FaithHome* from Abingdon Press. This 9-session experience helps families learn together how to talk to God and how to talk to one another about God and faith.

meeting today, but I said a prayer and God got me through it."

▲ Attend church together regularly. Afterward, talk about the things each of you learned and experienced. Get involved in fellowship and learning activities as well as service opportunities.

▲ Look for ways your family can work together to help others in your neighborhood and community and beyond. Make this a regular part of family life.

Recommended Resources

Books That Build Character: A Guide to Teaching Your Child Moral Values Through Stories by William Kirkpatrick and Gregory and Suzanne M. Wolfe (Simon and Schuster, 1994).

FaithHome Family Guide by Dan and Joy Solomon, Creators; Debra Ball-Kilbourne and MaryJane Pierce Norton, writers (Abingdon Press, 1997).

Family Time with God (Abingdon Press, October, 2001).

My Faith Journal by Karen Hill (Thomas Nelson, 1997).

Nurturing a Child's Soul by Timothy Jones (Word Publishing, 2000).

About the Author

Dr. James W. Moore is senior pastor of St. Luke's United Methodist Church in Houston and the author of numerous books, including *Seizing the Moments, Attitude Is Your Paintbrush, Some Folks Feel the Rain, Others Just Get Wet;* and *God Was Here and I Was Out to Lunch.*

FaithHome for Parents provides the church community with resources to support families and help children *to increase their faith, confirm their hope, and perfect them in love.*

0-687-04902-4

Your Child and Respect

How to Teach Your Child the Concept of Respect

FaithHome for **Parents** ™

Gathering Time
(4-5 minutes)
Have a tape or CD player available. Play a recording of Aretha Franklin's "R-E-S-P-E-C-T" as the class members arrive.

Say:
Today we are going to talk about respect—how we give it, how we earn it, how we get it, whether we can demand it, how we can command it.

Prayer
Open with this prayer or one of your own:
O Lord, You are the Creator of all, and in you all life has its being. Teach us to see your image in each person we encounter. Help us to teach our children to have respect for others. And most of all, help us in all humility to be worthy of our children's respect, In your Name. Amen.

Scenario

(8 minutes)

Read the scenario from the booklet (the story printed in italics). Discuss this question in pairs: If you were Josh's mother, how would you have handled that? How do you respect the umpire?How do you respect Josh in this situation?

Say:

Jesus said in Matthew 5, "Words kill."Think for a moment. Remember words that were said to you that were hurtful. Remember words you said that you wish you could take back. Remember words you wish you had said.

What Can You Do

(5-8 minutes)

As much as you may wish you could implant a "respect chip" in your child's brain, you can't force him or her to be respectful. But here are things you can do to change your child's behavior.

As you discuss these paragraphs from the booklet, briefly list them on a chalkboard or newsprint.

▲ Be a good example
▲ Be patient

As he looks at the umpire following a questionable call in the division playoffs, eleven-year-old Josh throws down his baseball glove and screams, "You don't know what you're talking about!"

Josh's mother later expresses her confusion and hurt to a family counselor. "We've always tried to teach our kids to treat other people with consideration," she says. "They know the Golden Rule by heart. We've tried to teach them the way our parents taught us. I just don't understand this behavior. What can we do?"

Whether it's on the ball field, in the classroom, or at home, respect for adult authority has dropped to an all-time low among today's youth. Some blame the dip on society's expressed values, some fault the song lyrics on popular radio stations, and others accuse parents' own fears of disciplining their children.

The new sense of entitlement that children and adolescents portray offers their parents, teachers, coaches, and leaders a new challenge to earn and receive respect. Since no one can make children or teenagers respect parents, other authority figures, or even themselves, the responsibility for producing change rests on exemplary behavior of parents and other significant adults.

What Can You Do?

Recognizing that all you can control is your own efforts, what can you do to bring about change in your child's behavior? Here are a few suggestions:

▲ Be a good example by demonstrating respectful behavior toward your own child as well as others. Often children imitate the behaviors of their parents, whether good or bad.

▲ Know that the work you are beginning with your child will take time. Giving a child respect and modeling respectful behavior will produce results, but not immediately. Be patient and consistent in your efforts.

▲ Expect respectful behavior from your child, regardless of the particular situation or environment. Be consistent, clear, and specific as

2

you work with your child. Do not make vague requests or count on your child to make the right assumptions; instead, set clear expectations and boundaries for appropriate and desired behaviors. You'll want to look for a comfortable balance between your parental expectations and your natural desire for easy, peer-like interaction with your child.

▲ Let each day be a new beginning. Once you have corrected your child for disrespectful behavior, including appropriate consequences, allow your child to have a fresh start. Encourage your child to learn from mistakes and move forward.

▲ Remember that you cannot afford to base your estimate of your success as a parent on the social, academic, or verbal performance of your child. All you can do is manage your own behavior and set boundaries and examples for your child. Recognize that you may not receive appreciation and honor for the work you're doing now with your child until your child matures—and perhaps has children of her or his own.

Steps to Building Respect

As you strive to set a good example for your child, remember that there are many aspects of respect. You may find it helpful to keep the following "checklist" handy.

Regard. Offering unconditional, positive regard for your child shows that he or she matters to you. Making time to give your child your undivided attention will help your child to feel "My parent is concerned for me." Children rarely respect a parent if they don't feel the parent respects them. Helping your child feel valued will cause him or her to develop self-confidence. Assuring your child of her or his worth can help to increase your child's ability to make acceptable choices and decrease her or his self-deprecating behaviors and hurtful language.

Positive speech. Children often "run" from conversations with their parents because they

▲ Have consistent expectations
▲ Start fresh each day
▲ Wait for your rewards

Teacher note:
"Setting boundaries" may be a new term to some parents. It means setting limits, putting a fence around how far you will let your child go. Boundaries determine when a behavior is "out of bounds."

Boundaries can also be emotional. A boundary separates you from your child: you are two distinct individuals; therefore, you can only control your own behavior and emotions. You can set an example for your child, but you can't control his feelings.

Steps to Building Respect
(10-15 minutes)
Divide the class into small groups. Assign each group one of the five steps to discuss.

▲ Regard: I care about you.
▲ Positive Speech: I respect you.
▲ Sensitive listening: I hear you.
▲ Acceptable compromise: I will work with you.

3

Ask each group to think of a situation where each step could be utilized. Allow each group to explain their step and describe the sample situation.

want to avoid being talked to, put down, or preached to. Avoid harsh and emotionally charged remarks, such as "Your attitude is going to make me have a heart attack!" and "I'll be surprised if you don't end up in prison." Refrain from saying anything that will lead to feelings of resentment or hate. Everything you say to your child should encourage connection. Children who hear positive speech learn positive speech.

Sensitive listening. Take time to listen to your child. Let your child know that you understand his or her feelings before you offer advice or instruction. Children experience frustration and resentment when parents seem indifferent to their thoughts and feelings. When a child is in the middle of a crisis or a strong emotional reaction, he or she wants to be understood without having to divulge everything that he or she is experiencing. Remember, dismissing a child's emotions will cause the child to assume that most of his or her views are inferior and unwanted. Listening to your child will help him or her to feel empowered.

Acceptable compromise. Share your thoughts and ideas with your child without belittling your child. Approaching each issue or confrontation with the "I've-got-to-win" mentality almost always results in a battle. Remember that children have more energy than parents and can argue without end— because winning is everything to them, too! Using a give-and-take approach will begin to result in acceptable compromises. This type of conversation isn't defensive or angry. It ensures a reasonable form of win-win.

Consideration. Engage your child in healthy conversations by always being willing to consider the truth of what he or she is saying—even those statements you may find personally hurtful. This openness will allow you to accept the truth of what was said and respond appropriately. Too often we react defensively to the dis-

4

respectful reactions of our children. Cutting off a real discussion can result in an unproductive standoff. Consider the truth, and don't let your child's emotions hinder quality communication even if it seems disrespectful to you.

Correcting Disrespectful Behavior Now

Your child may be exhibiting some behaviors that you need to stop immediately. If so, you need a simple plan that you can enact consistently whenever disrespectful behavior occurs. For best results, tell your child about the plan in a clear and unemotional way. Children should feel that they are in control of the positive or negative outcome of their behavior. Revise the following plan as necessary to fit your own situation and needs:

▲ When alone, stop and think about what changes you would like to see in your child's behavior. Make a list of desired behaviors and a list of unacceptable behaviors. Try to be as specific as possible.

▲ Determine consequences for the unacceptable behaviors. The consequences should be clear and specific and should allow your child to learn from his or her mistakes. Then focus on finding ways to help your child recognize the desired behaviors and receive recognition for demonstrating them. Some parents use a "reward system" in which specific bad

Children should feel that they are in control of the positive or negative outcome of their behavior.

5

Correcting Disrespectful Behavior

(8-10 minutes)

As you discuss this section, remind parents that they will want to adapt this plan to suit the age of their child. Very young children will need gentle reminders about the rules of society, rather than a complicated system of consequences for unacceptable behaviors.

Outlining this section visually will help it have more impact. Write on a chalkboard or newsprint

▲ Behaviors to change
▲ Consequence for each behavior
▲ Discuss with child
▲ Follow through

Everyone, young and old, responds well to praise when they do something right. Urge parents to remember to praise their child often, when he does something right, or even when he doesn't do something wrong! ("You were very quiet while I talked to Mrs. Jones, Tina. Thank you for not interrupting.") A positive is always more persuasive than a negative.

When to Seek Additional Help

(3-4 minutes)

Alert parents that working with children takes time. If after several months you see little progress you may want to seek additional help. Review the signals that more help is needed:

▲ Child makes no adjustments

▲ Nothing works

▲ Outbursts/mood swings

▲ Threatens harm

▲ Words/actions interfere with development

▲ Continually disruptive behavior

behaviors result in lost privileges while good behaviors result in verbal praise or special privileges. Keeping a "score card" on the refrigerator and "tallying" behaviors for a week is one way to keep track. Wait for a predetermined number of negative behaviors before enforcing a consequence, so that the child has room to learn. Remember, there are varying ways to encourage behavioral changes, and you will want to find the method that best meets your child's needs.

▲ Outline both the desired and unacceptable behaviors to your child. For each behavior, talk about how the rest of the family and/or others feel when your child behaves this way. Reaffirm how pleasant it is to be with your child when she or he is demonstrating the desired behaviors, as opposed to the unacceptable behaviors. Then discuss the ways you plan to respond to both desired and unacceptable behaviors. Be clear about specific consequences for unacceptable behaviors; the "rules" must be very clear. Expect to answer a lot of very specific questions from your child about how the plan will work.

▲ Once everyone understands the plan, follow through! Be prepared to recognize and respond to behaviors when they happen.

When to Seek Additional Help

As with anything requiring your consistent effort, it takes time to bring about change. If you know you have a child with a strong will, it may take a little while longer to see results. Don't give up. If things do not improve in time, you may need to seek additional help. Here are some signals to look for:

▲ Your child chooses to make no adjustments.

▲ You have tried everything you know to try and nothing has worked.

▲ Your child has regular, uncontrollable emotional outbursts or mood swings.

▲ Your child has threatened to harm self or others. (Verbal threats can be deadly warnings. Let your child know that you will assume he or she is serious about any threat.)

6

▲ Your child's actions or words interfere with social, academic, family, and/or spiritual development.
▲ Your child's behaviors are continually disruptive to the family.

A pastor or family ministries professional can give you a referral or recommendation for a good family counselor. Remember to approach counseling as a family matter and not the problem of one family member. (To find a licensed family therapist in your area, you might try the online directory at www.aamft.org.)

The Faith Perspective

We respect what we judge to have worth. As Christians we believe that every human being is created in God's image. That makes a difference in how we react and respond in daily life. Do we view the slow checker at the grocery store as a person we greet and look at eye-to-eye or do our children see us treat the others who serve us as invisible? Do we speak politely to the police officer who pulls us over for running a red light and then spout all sorts of names while driving away as our kids listen from the backseat? Do we speak to our spouses and children as if we are talking to people with sacred worth? Our task as parents is to help our children understand that the umpire who makes a questionable call during a baseball game is a person of sacred worth who deserves to have his authority respected when he has been given the job of making close calls. We can teach our children to value their own opinions and views while offering others respect simply because they are God's creations.

Jesus clearly tells us in Matthew that both words and actions convey our respect toward others. He says, "You're familiar with the command to the ancients, 'Do not murder.' I'm telling you that anyone who is so much as angry with a brother or sister is guilty of murder. Carelessly call a brother 'idiot!' and you just might find yourself hauled into court.

7

Faith Perspective
(3-4 minutes)
Read the Scripture from Matthew 5:22-23 (*The Message*).

Ask:
Did this translation startle you? It sounds much more blunt to our ears than other translations of Jesus' sayings. Jesus was dead serious about this issue of respect. He talked about anger and name-calling in terms of the law and the court system. But he also added the psychological and spiritual aspects as well:
▲ Words kill.
▲ Words kill exuberance, confidence, joy.
▲ Words kill the heart, the spirit, the soul.

Assignment
Create a grade card for yourself for this week. List the five steps:
▲ Regard
▲ Positive Speech
▲ Sensitive listening
▲ Acceptable compromise
▲ Consideration
Give yourself a grade for how you did each day in each area. If you didn't use a particular step on a given day, give yourself a star instead of a grade to remind you to use it tomorrow!

Close with this prayer, or one of your own:
O Lord, Help us to respect our children as sacred trusts from You. And guide us as we seek to teach them to respect others. Amen

Thoughtlessly yell 'stupid!' at a sister and you are on the brink of hellfire. The simple moral fact is that words kill" (*Matthew* 5:22-23 from *The Message*).

Today make it a goal to remind your children that they and all they will meet are made by God. There is the spark of God in everyone.

Recommended Resources

Books That Build Character: A Guide to Teaching Your Child Moral Values Through Stories, by William Kilpatrick and Gregory and Suzanne M. Wolfe (Simon & Schuster, 1994).

Changing Your Child's Heart, by Steve Sherbondy (Tyndale House Publishers, 1998).

501 Practical Ways to Teach Your Children Values, Bobbie Reed (Concordia Publishing House, 1998).

Raising Good Children, by Thomas Lickona (Bantam Books, 1994).

For more resources visit www.FaithHome.com

About the Author

D. Tony Rankin parents with his wife, Amber. They have three children: Drew, Caleb, and Katelin. When he's not parenting, coaching baseball, or dancing with his daughter at her recitals, he is the director and clinical therapist of The Counseling Center in Nashville, Tennessee. In addition to numerous advice columns and magazine articles, he is the author of *When True Love Doesn't Wait*. He enjoys speaking at seminars and conventions and has taught as an adjunct instructor in psychology and religion at Belmont University.

Scripture taken from *The Message*, Copyright © by Eugene H. Peterson, 1993, 1994, 1995. Used by permission of NavPress Publishing Group.

FaithHome for Parents provides the church community with resources to support families and help children *to increase their faith, confirm their hope, and perfect them in love.*

ISBN 068708879-8

Your Child and Discipline

Gaining Cooperation so that Everybody Wins

FaithHome for Parents™

Gathering Time
(5-8 minutes)

On a table in your meeting space, place a container of modeling clay or Play-Doh™ for every two people. As class members arrive, invite them to take a piece of clay and shape it into whatever they like. Ask them to leave their creations on display until you tell them to put the clay away.

Prayer
(1-2 minutes)

Begin with this prayer or one of your own:

O Lord, you shaped us in your image. Help us to mold our children into healthy, faithful disciples of your will and your way. Give us loving hands and patient spirits, in the name of Jesus, the Christ. Amen.

Say:

You have been working with clay—shaping it, squeezing it, pushing it, changing it from a shapeless blob into something that you envisioned. It was pliable and easy to work with, but if we leave it alone, what will happen to it?

We are going to talk in this session about what we envision for our children and the ways we shape them toward that goal.

Scenario
(4-5 minutes)
Read the scenario from the booklet (the story printed in italics). Divide the class into two groups. Assign one group the situation with Shannon and Nicholas, and the other group, Hayes. Ask them to consider these questions:

▲ Of the possible parental responses suggested, which do you recommend?

▲ What do each of the suggested responses teach the child or children involved?

(Keep in mind the ages of the children!)

Have the class put away their Play-Doh.

Improving Behavior
(30-35 minutes)
Say:
Discipline comes from the same root word as disciple; both mean to teach or train. Discipline is not punishment; it is training for life.

Ten-year-old Shannon and her brother Nicholas, age six, are fighting again. Do you tell them they can't watch television tonight, offer them $1.00 each to stop or put them on separate ends of the couch and tell them they can get up when they give each other permission?

Hayes, age three, rides his tricycle into the street. Do you scold him, spank him, or remove the tricycle and watch him more closely?

Discipline—before we can do it, we need to understand what it is. Most of us have been taught that discipline is merely changing or improving our children's behavior. This view of discipline is short-sighted because it deals only with current behavior—the behavior of the moment—and allows the same misbehavior to reoccur again and again. It misses the less obvious but critical long-term effects of discipline.

What we often overlook is that the root word of discipline means *to teach*. We must recognize that the way we discipline our children affects not only their current behavior but also their future behavior. In addition to teaching life skills such as problem solving, anger management, personal responsibility, and respectful language, effective discipline teaches life lessons and guiding life principles—principles that our children will use for the rest of their lives when making decisions and choosing their behavior.

Every disciplinary action we take is grounded in a principle that, whether we are aware of it or not, will be learned and later used by our children. This is why it is important that we use disciplinary techniques that not only will effectively alter behavior but also will teach principles that will be helpful to our children as they mature into adolescence and adulthood. The goal for all discipline, after all, is to lead to self-discipline.

Improving Your Child's Behavior While Teaching Valuable Life Principles
Using disciplinary techniques that effectively improve behavior and teach helpful life principles will allow you to maintain your own integrity by practicing principles in which you

2

trongly believe, such as the Golden Rule,
espect, and honesty. Here are some common
areas requiring discipline and specific techniques
you can use to address them:

Spills, Messes, Broken Toys, and Hurt Feelings

Did you know that how you respond when
your two-year-old spills juice actually will determine his or her behavior in the years to come?
Guiding your child to make remedy and amends
when he is young helps teach lifelong responsibility and consideration for others. Let's consider
the spilled juice example.

First of all, remember that when your young
child makes a mess; such as spilling juice, you
should not take it personally. Most likely, the
mess is either an accident or the result of inno-
cent play, rather than an attempt to irritate you.
Not getting angry at misbehavior helps us to
handle ourselves more respectfully.

Since a young toddler is unable to clean up a
spill without help, you can send your child to
get a cloth or sponge for cleanup. By age three,
you can teach your child to wet the cloth and
then wring it out; by age four, to wipe up the
spill; and by age five, to rinse and wring the
cloth again and clean the area a second time.
Yes, your child has learned how to clean up a
liquid mess; but even more importantly, he or
she has learned that when you make a mess—or
break things, or "undo" things—it is your
responsibility to put things back the way they
were.

Here are two important things to remember
about lessons: (1) your child will continue to
give you opportunities to teach a particular lesson until he or she learns it, and (2) your child
will learn the lesson, but at his or her own
speed. You cannot know how many lessons your
child will require; you can know, however, that if
you persistently teach a lesson, your child eventually will learn the concept. You will know your
child has learned this particular lesson when he
or she initiates action to make amends in a particular situation.

Let's say that several years after the spilled
juice incident your child goes to a friend's

3

Write on a chalkboard or
newsprint:
Discipline teaches:
▲ problem solving
▲ anger management
▲ personal responsibility
▲ respectful language
▲ decision making skills
▲ principles for choosing
   behavior

Spills, Messes, Broken Toys, and Hurt Feelings

A simple lesson of responsibility—cleaning up spilled
juice—is the first step of a
long journey of training.
Take this section step by
step, remembering that the
child is not being punished
for spilling the juice. He is
being trained to take
responsibility and to make
amends. He is learning to
put things back like they
were. Gradually, the lesson
is learned, and the child
disciplines himself. He
makes amends without
being reminded by a par-
ent.

Be sure to note the last
paragraph of this section,
which applies this same
technique to other situa-
tions, such as interpersonal
relationships.

Picking up Toys, Clothes, Etc.

Take this section age by age. Notice how teaching occurs in stages. The competence learned in this process is cumulative and results in good decision making skills for life.

Do not miss the learning for parents in the section called "All Ages."

Key Points

▲ Twos—Habit and routine can build desired behaviors

▲ Threes—Make it fun

▲ Fours—Create expectations with simple rules

▲ Fives and older—Introduce consequences

▲ Eleven and older–choose your battles

house, plays with a toy, and accidentally breaks it. Then, without any intervention from a grown-up, your child expresses a desire to replace the broken item—perhaps offering to take money out of his or her own piggy bank to buy a new toy. No need for discipline. Actually, that is not quite true. Discipline most certainly has taken place. It's called self-discipline, and you began teaching it when your child was two years old and spilled juice. Not a bad investment!

Remedy and amends is also a good technique to use when your child says or does mean things to another child or physically hurts another child. As the children play together, have your child make amends by playing what the other child wants to play. The lesson here is that when you make someone feel bad, your job is to help that person feel better.

Picking up Toys, Clothes, Etc.

Two-Year-Olds: Habit and Routine

Preschool teachers know how to get two-year-olds to clean up: they sing a song and model the desired behavior. Parents often ask me, "What song?" Any song will do as long as it's always the same song. The technique is called habit and routine. Habit either will be your best friend or your worst enemy. If you wait to take action until after you've lost your patience and yelled at your child, your habit will teach your child not to do anything until you are angry and yelling. But if you take action after you speak the first time, you teach your child to listen when you talk. The choice is up to you.

Three-Year-Olds: Outsmart Them

One of the most helpful strategies to use with preschoolers is to outsmart them and make things fun. Have your three-year-old try to clean up before a timer goes off. Or use forced choice: "Do you want to pick up the blocks or the books?" Pretend you are a crane and swing your child around to grab books and toys to put away.

4

Four-Year-Olds: Use a Rule

Use a simple rule: If you play, you pick up. Any self-respecting four-year-old will complain, "But I don't want to." Don't get angry. Simply pause, and then say, "It is your responsibility to pick up after playing. When you play, you pick up."

Five and Older: Disciplinary Consequences

Explain this concept: After you pick up, then you may go on with your life. "Go on with your life" means anything your child may want to do, such as go to practice, play with friends, play alone, talk on the phone, eat a snack, and so forth. This teaches doing first things first.

Eleven and Older: Close the Door

By the preteen years, a child's room should become his or her own. With the possible exception of cleaning days when a child needs to pick up his or her room so that it can be cleaned (if this is not his or her chore), simply allow the room to be kept however your child chooses. You want your preteen to feel that his or her room is a haven. This concession will allow the child a safe form of rebellion that may help keep her from turning to more dangerous rebellious activities like experimentation with drugs or alcohol.

All Ages

If you are resentful about things you feel you no longer should have to do for your child, such as picking up toys, listen to your heart. Stop doing those things. Lose the resentment. Resentment can be our friend; it tells us when we are acting foolishly.

Tantrums

How many times has your two- or three-year-old yelled, "I hate you," or thrown herself on the ground when she didn't get what she wanted? There are two steps to help your child through this strong expression of emotion.

The first step is to help her calm down by holding or rocking her if she will allow this. If not, stay near her but allow her space and time to bring herself back to calmness. Ignoring her, traditionally suggested, often leads to escalated

5

Tantrums

Every parent has suffered the embarrassment of a toddler's public tantrum. Here is what not to do, and a two-step plan to teach the child that tantrums just aren't worth the effort they require.

Tip for All Ages

Know when to stop doing things for your child that he or she can do for themselves.

An Ounce of Prevention
It can be helpful to point out to children that everyone in the family lives with the same job description, that is, everyone is expected to live up to the same code:

▲ Be respectful
▲ Be nice
▲ Be helpful

Reaching for and Getting Long-term Results

How you deal with your children early will net you long-term results. Using discipline that teaches guiding principles assures that you will reap the rewards of children who have learned to self-discipline.

behavior, which may include hurting things, others or self.

After you have helped your child return to peacefulness immediately following a tantrum, it is time for step two. This involves taking your child back to the situation that started the tantrum and doing discipline or problem solving. For example, if your child refused to pick up toys, you would return her to the toys that still need to be picked up. The worst thing we can do is pick up the toys for her. This teaches a child that tantrums work, that they get you what you want. This is not a lesson we want to teach.

Again, the two steps in dealing with temper tantrums to remember are:

▲ Help the child calm down. Rock, hold, hum, give time and space.
▲ Return to the issue and discipline or problem solve.

An Ounce of Prevention

Teach your child that every member of the family has the same job description:

1. It is your job to get along with other family members. You may disagree with someone, but you must do it in an agreeable manner. (Note: You will have to model getting-along skills and teach problem-solving skills, anger management, and respectful language. You cannot expect your children to intuitively know how to do these things.)
Be respectful.

2. It is your job to help others in the family feel valued and appreciated.
Be nice.

3. It is your job to contribute to the maintenance and progress of the family.
Be helpful.

Reaching for and Getting Long-Term Results

Years ago, as a mother of young children, I thought that my two-year-old would need lots of discipline. I was right. I also thought that my five-year-old should require less discipline, being three years older. After all, those three years should have netted something positive.

6

If we use disciplinary techniques that teach lessons and guiding principles, our children will require less and less discipline as they age. For one thing, they will be acquiring more and more skills. Even more important, they will be learning more and more life lessons and will be grounding themselves in helpful principles, not flawed ones.

Know those principles you are teaching your child, for those principles will return to help or haunt in the years ahead.

When to Seek Additional Help

▲ Seek help if it becomes difficult for you to think of anything you like about your child, even when he or she is asleep.

▲ Seek help if your child is behaving in a way that is radically different from his or her peer group. Have tolerance for minor variances from the norm.

▲ Seek help if your child changes behavior patterns or temperament suddenly or dramatically and the change continues.

▲ Seek help if your child becomes violent, withdrawn, destructive, or abusive. (You can find excellent resources at your local library offering discipline techniques for handling minor verbal and physical aggression and sibling rivalry.)

▲ Seek help if you are abusive or have difficulty controlling angry reactions.

▲ Seek help if you feel lost or inadequate as a parent. Talk to other parents you respect, your child's teacher, and/or a pastor or family counselor.

▲ Read parenting books and seek advice from competent and experienced parenting advisors.

The Faith Perspective
Ephesians 6:4
Do not provoke your children to anger, but bring them up in the discipline and instruction of the Lord. (NRSV)

A disciple is one who follows after another who is wise and more skilled. Take your children by the hand and lead them in the ways of God. Show them rather than tell them what is good, right, and pleasing in God's sight.

7

When to Seek Additional Help

These important guidelines are a mixture; some are for children who are out of control. Others are for parents who are at or near the edge. Allow class members to ask questions or offer support to each other. Have available a hotline number for abuse prevention (look in the yellow pages under Human Services Organizations). A qualified family therapist can be found on the database at www.aamft.org.

Say:
Raising children is hard work. It is understandable that occasionally you need reinforcements. Don't hesitate to ask for help.

The Faith Perspective
(4-5 minutes)
Read aloud Ephesians 6:4.

When you fly on commercial airlines, you are instructed in the proper use of oxygen masks. One of the directions given is to persons traveling with small children: "If you are traveling with small children, place your oxygen mask over your face first, then assist the child with his."

The reason, of course, is that you cannot help your child if you are unconscious.

The same is true of teaching your child how to live a disciplined life. You must have your own skills in place before you can teach your child "in the discipline and instruction of the Lord."

To lead our children in the ways of God means that we must first know and follow those ways ourselves. The greatest help a parent can find is available through prayer. Encourage your students to pray for their children daily and to pray for their own parenting skills.

Closing Prayer
Close with this prayer or one of your own:
O Lord, turn our faces toward you, That we may learn to follow you, And lead our children in your ways. Amen.

Recommended Resources

Discipline for Life: Getting it Right with Children, by Madelyn Swift (Stairway Education Programs, 1998).

Boundaries With Kids: When to Say Yes, When to Say No to Help Your Children Gain Control of Their Lives, by Henry Cloud and John Townsend (Zondervan Publishing House, 1998).

Raising Good Children, by Thomas Lickona (Bantam Doubleday Dell Publishing, 1994).

10 Most Common Mistakes Good Parents Make: And How to Avoid Them, by Kevin Steede, Ph.D. (Prima Publishing, 1998).

The Parent Lifesaver: Practical Help for Everyday Childhood Problems, by Todd Cartmell (Baker Book House, 1998).

Time-In: When Time-Out Doesn't Work, by Jean Illsley Clarke (Parenting Press, 1999).

For more resources visit www.FaithHome.com.

About the Author

Madelyn Swift, M.Ed., is a nationally acclaimed author, speaker, and authority on discipline, family dynamics, and personal communication. Madelyn is president of Childright, an educational consulting firm that provides training to educators, administrators, parents, and corporations. She is the author of *Discipline for Life: Getting it Right with Children* and is currently completing her third book. Madelyn completed her Master of Education degree at Bowling Green State University and her certification as a school psychologist from the State of Ohio.

FaithHome for Parents provides the church community with resources to support families and help children *to increase their faith, confirm their hope, and perfect them in love.*

Copyright © 1999 by Madelyn Swift.
Used by permission of the author. All rights reserved.
Produced by Abingdon Press.
1-800-672-1789
ISBN 068708889-5

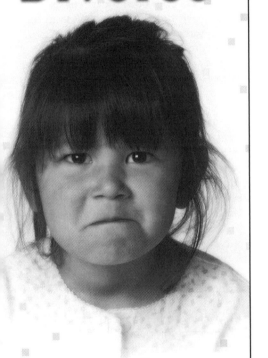

Helping Your Child Cope with Divorce

Children Need Special Attention to Feel Secure Through Such a Major Life Transition

Gathering Time
(4-5 minutes)
Have paper and pens or pencils available for everyone. As people arrive, ask them to write down one piece of advice they would give any parent going through a divorce. These will be used later in the session.

Prayer
Begin with this prayer or one of your own:
O Lord, We live in a fallen, broken world, And sometimes that brokenness extends into our families. We ask your forgiveness, And ask you to remove our burden of guilt. Help us to love our children, soothe their grief, and lay to rest their fears, through your love and power. Amen.

Scenario

(2-3 minutes)
Read the scenario from the booklet (the story printed in italics).

Ask:

Does this sound familiar? Why do you think children try to assume responsibility for the divorce?

Say:

Divorce is like a hurricane: you may see it coming, but that doesn't make it easy to withstand. In this session we will discuss ways for you to cope and ways to help your children through the most confusing crisis they will face.

Stages of Grief

The introduction lists many predictable reactions a child will experience. They are natural and should not cause undue alarm, unless they do not abate with time.

The stages of grief are listed in the order they commonly occur; however, the progression through them is not clean and precise. You may think you (or your child) are through with denial and bargaining only to find yourself right back in that mode. Be assured that gradually you will

"Michele, your room is a mess!" Sharon said crossly. "For the third time, go clean up your room or you won't like the consequences!"

Eight-year-old Michele looked up at her mother and began crying uncontrollably. Concerned, Sharon gathered Michele into her arms and comforted her, murmuring soothingly, "I love you, Michele. What's the matter?"

"That's why Daddy left, isn't it? Because I didn't clean my room?"

Sharon sobbed.

Many children born today will spend at least a part of their growing-up years in a single-parent home. Some researchers claim the figure to be as high as one in three. A significant percentage of these will be children of divorced parents.

Virtually all children assume some level of blame for the divorce of their parents. They believe that if they had been better students, kept their room cleaner, or stopped fighting with siblings, the divorce never would have occurred. In addition to feelings of guilt, children also experience the same stages of grief as adults: shock, denial, bargaining, sadness, depression, anger, powerlessness, a sense of rejection, abandonment, isolation, and finally acceptance and hope. They may respond to the early stages of grief by withdrawing, regressing to an earlier childhood stage, striking back with aggression, failing in school, giving up on themselves, losing interest in everything, experiencing moodiness or lethargy, having physical pain and illness, or becoming increasingly demanding of physical contact. They may go through times when they want to live with the other parent, or with grandparents, because they are so unhappy in their own home and think that things would be better someplace else—anyplace else! They often experience exaggerated fears of rejection and abandonment. Most

2

of the time these reactions diminish as children work through the grieving process.

Ways You Can Help Ease the Pain

None of us wants our children to hurt. We want to protect them from harm in every way. Yet divorce does hurt children. There doesn't seem to be any age at which it is easier for a child to handle a divorce. Divorce is difficult for children of any age—up to adulthood. Older and adult children have the ability to understand what's happening on a cognitive level, even if they still feel pain and anger; younger children find the entire situation confusing, frustrating, upsetting, and painful.

As a parent, you can help your child feel more secure and loved and, therefore, a little less distraught. Here are some suggestions.

Overcoming the fear that your child will "lose" you too:

▲ Keep your word. If you say you will be at your child's ball game, be there. If you say you will be coming home at 6:00 P.M., be on time.

▲ Always let your child know where you are and how you can be reached by telephone, beeper, or cell phone.

▲ For a younger child, allow a night-light in the bedroom or hallway.

Easing the longing for the other parent:

▲ Encourage your child to telephone the other parent, pray for the other parent, and have photos of the other parent in her or his room.

▲ Prepare stamped envelopes addressed to the other parent so that your child can write whenever he or she chooses. Have a younger child dictate the letter while you write. Give a teenager stamps, stationery, and a personal address book including the other parent's address(es)—mailing address and, if applicable, e-mail address—and phone number.

3

work your way through them and be done. The stages are:

Shock
Denial
Bargaining
Sadness
Depression
Anger
Powerlessness
Rejection
Abandonment
Isolation
Acceptance
Hope

Ways You Can Help Ease the Pain

(20 minutes)

Your child will be hurt by your divorce. You will be hurting too, and it is difficult to help someone else's pain in the midst of your own.

Discuss the steps under each of these categories: There are things you can do. For each, consider the list of suggestions in the booklet. Are there any other ideas?

▲ Overcome the fear of abandonment.
A child's secure world is shattered by the departure of one parent. These are ways to reassure him that he can depend on you.

▲ Ease the longing for the other parent.
As much as possible, allow access to the other parent. Parents divorce each other, not their kids.

▲ Remember, the child is always missing someone. When he is with you, he misses the other parent, and vice versa. Allow the child to keep his happy memories from the intact family--pictures, keepsakes, gifts. They are part of his life.

▲ Making visitation a pleasant experience.
Until your child is an adult, you and his other parent will have to cooperate in a business-like, if not cordial, manner. Respect the other parent's rights. Learn to be empathetic: "How would I feel if he did this to me?"

▲ Build up your child's esteem.
You cannot tell your child too often that you love her and that she is important to you.

▲ Providing a dependable structure.
Surprises are not always fun when life feels uncertain. Make things predictable for a while.

After you have briefly dis-

▲ Tell the child in what (positive) ways she or he reminds you of the other parent.
Making visitation a pleasant experience:
▲ Have the child ready for visits on time with the appropriate clothes or equipment (swimwear, jackets, etc.).
▲ Do not turn pick-up and drop-off times into forums for arguing and attacking the other parent.
▲ Understand that sometimes emergency situations do arise that will change visitation plans.
▲ Do not change visitation plans capriciously.
▲ Do not expect the child to "spy" for you.

Building up your child's esteem:
▲ Catch your child doing well or being good and give a sincere compliment.

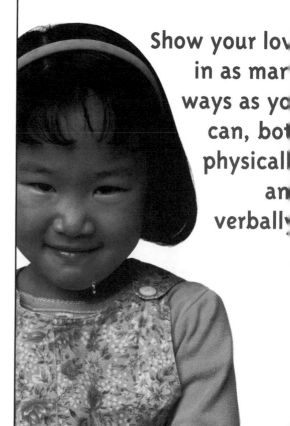

Show your lov
in as mar
ways as yo
can, bot
physicall
an
verball

▲ Spend time doing things together, and let your child choose the activities.
▲ Ask for, listen to, and consider your child's input on family decisions.
▲ Don't criticize or belittle the other parent.
▲ Give your child responsibilities at home so that she or he can contribute and feel competent.
▲ Teach your child how to do a task correctly, but don't come along behind and redo what your child has done. (The message that gives is "You really can't do it!")
▲ Share your pride in your child's accomplishments with your friends—in front of your child.
▲ Avoid using derogatory labels when addressing your child. Never call your child stupid, dumb, lazy, clumsy, or crazy.
▲ Show your love in as many ways as you can, both physically and verbally.
▲ Teach your child about God's unconditional love. Pray and read the Bible together.

Providing a dependable structure:
▲ Make, communicate, and consistently enforce reasonable family rules.
▲ Establish a workable daily schedule so that your child knows what he or she is supposed to be doing when (chores, homework, playing, or listening to music). Don't forget to build some "free time" into the schedule, and allow for some flexibility.
▲ Be consistent in your relationship with your child. Don't laugh at a behavior today and scream at your child tomorrow for the same behavior.
▲ Attend church each week with your child.

Taking these steps not only brings results in the specific categories named but also has

5

cussed these, have the class take a few minutes to decide what things they are doing well and which they need to work on.

If your family isn't experiencing divorce
▲ What can you do to help other families?
▲ Do you see suggestions that family and friends can help accomplish.

How to Get Help for Your Child
(5 minutes)

Several of these suggestions are actually help for the parent, which, of course, also helps the child. Find out where a divorce recovery group is available in your area. If there is none available, perhaps your class would like to begin one.

Even if the child seems to be doing fine, it is a good idea for her to have another trusted and objective adult she can talk to. The parent also needs a good friend to talk to—some one other than the child to share negative feelings or comments.

Don't Give Up
(5 minutes)

Many counselors say that the most reliable predictor for how a child will adjust to the divorce is how well the custodial parent adjusts. It helps to keep your eye on the ultimate goal: ideally a child needs a strong, healthy relationship with both his mother and his father. Keep your own anger out of the way of that developing relationship.

Other Hints
Invite class members to share the advice they wrote down at the Gathering

a secondary effect of improving a child's behavior habits.

How To Get Help for Your Child
Sometimes a child needs more help for getting through the grieving cycle following a divorce than you are able to give. In that case, you might consider these suggestions:

▲ Find a church-based divorce recovery program that is designed with components for both adults and children.
▲ Attend one or more parenting seminars for divorced parents.
▲ Read a couple of good Christian books on the subject of divorce and children. (See the following list of suggested resources.)
▲ Consider sending your child to a church-based school.
▲ Inquire if your church or community has a big brother/sister program.
▲ Ask a pastor or family ministries professional for a referral to a good Christian counselor.

Don't Give Up
Remember that a single-parent family can be a happy, healthy family. A survey of adults who had been raised by single parents revealed that there were three things that influenced whether or not the experience was positive:

▲ The attitude of the single parent toward the situation. If the parent had a positive attitude, so did the child.
▲ The attitude of the custodial single parent toward the other parent. Children who were free to love and to contact the other parent had a better growing-up experience.
▲ The quality of the time spent with the child. The quantity of time spent together was less significant, as long as

6

they had a good, loving time and felt good about themselves when they were together. Remember to be flexible. Sometimes you need to relax the rules and be merciful and forgiving. Let the schedule slip and the deadlines go by. In the eternal scheme of time, family relationships are more important than tasks, deadlines, projects, chores, preferences, and schedules.

▲ Even on the worst days, don't give up. If you can keep a sense of humor, today's disasters may become tomorrow's favorite stories.

The Faith Perspective
Romans 8: 35, 37
Who will separate us from the love of Christ? Will hardship, or distress, or persecution, or famine, or nakedness, or peril, or sword?

No, in all these things we are more than conquerors through him who loved us. (NRSV)

Ephesians 2:14
For he is our peace; in his flesh he has made both groups into one and has broken down the dividing wall, that is, the hostility between us. (NRSV)

Through the separation and hardships that divorce brings on families, God's love is ever-present. While the couple may be divided and apart, the child's relationship as family with both adults may be able to be maintained. Ephesians 2: 13-22 offers hope that, through God's love and strength, we may be able to keep the hostility diminished so that children can freely love and appreciate both parents.

Time.

The Faith Perspective
(5 minutes)
Read Romans 8: 35, 37 and Ephesians 2:14. Emphasize that God's love surrounds us and sustains us. Hard as it may be to believe now, God will break down the hostility between you. Never underestimate the power of prayer. Your faith community can provide an extended family if your own relatives are far away. Opportunities for social contact in Sunday school and church are healthy for parent and child.

Your Assignment
(2-3 minutes)
If there was one aspect of "Ways You can Help Ease the Pain" that you identified as a real need, discipline yourself to work on that this week.

Close with this prayer or one of your own:
O God of new beginnings, Heal our hearts and spirits. Help us to claim your promise to make all things new. We hold our children before you and ask your blessings on them in the name of Christ. Amen.

7

Resources

For Reading with Children

Dinosaurs Divorce: A Guide for Changing Families, by Marc Tolon Brown/Laurence Krasny Brown (Little Brown & Co, 1986).

Why Don't We Live Together Anymore? Understanding Divorce, by Robin Prince Monroe (Concordia Publishing House, 1998).

For Adults

Be a Great Divorced Dad, Dr. Kenneth N.Condrell/Linda Lee Small, Contributor (St. Martin's Griffin, 1998).

Breaking & Mending: Divorce and God's Grace, Mary L. Redding (Upper Room, 1998).

Children of Divorce, by Debbie Barr (Zondervan Publishing House, 1992).

Divorced Kids: What You Need to Know to Help Kids Survive a Divorce, by Laurene Johnson/ Georglyn Rosenfeld (Fawcett Crest, 1992).

Growing Through Divorce, by Jim Smoke (Harvest House Publishers, Inc., 1995).

For more resources visit www.FaithHome.com.

About the Author

Bobbie Reed has a Ph.D. in social psychology and a Doctor of Ministry degree with a specialty in single adult ministry. After ten years of marriage, Bobbie was divorced and became a single parent for ten years, during which time her two sons had two stepmothers. When Bobbie married again, she became a stepmother of two adult children. In the last twenty-seven years, she has, in addition to holding a full-time job, served as a mother, wife, lecturer, consultant, conference speaker, college professor and author of thirty-six books. She and her husband, Ed, are ministers with single adults at Skyline Wesleyan Church in Lemon Grove, California.

FaithHome for Parents provides the church community with resources to support families and help children *to increase their faith, confirm their hope, and perfect them in love.*

Helping Your Child Cope with Grief

Supporting Your Child Through Grief and Loss

Gathering Time

(5 minutes)

Have a piece of cloth about 4" x 8" for each member of the class. (Buy a remnant at a cloth or craft shop, or use leftover fabric from home). As persons arrive, give them a piece of cloth and ask them to tear it into two pieces, then think of a useful or decorative function for their pieces. Invite them to share in twos or threes what they could do with their remnants, and, if they wish, tell briefly about the first time they lost a loved one to death.

Prayer

(1-2 minutes)

Begin with this prayer or one of your own:

Lord of Life, The danger of loving is losing, and there comes a time when each of us will lose someone we love. Comfort us when we grieve, And strengthen us so that we may comfort our children. Guide us in that time, in the name of Jesus Christ who conquered death for all time. Amen.

Scenario

(5 minutes)

Read the scenario from the booklet (the story printed in italics).

Say:

Aaron, Kate and Mom have just had their lives ripped apart, just as you tore the cloth in your hands. It won't ever again be just like it was before. They have to find a way to adjust, to adapt, to function in a new way, just as you searched for a new purpose for your torn cloth.

Ask:

Besides the loss of their father, what other losses have Aaron and Kate sustained? (The loss of their security and, for a time, a happy, stable mom.)
Besides the loss of her husband, what other losses has their mother suffered? (Among many others, the loss of security, income, and temporarily at least, well-adjusted, happy children.)

Understanding How Children Grieve

Another reason for a child's intermittent expression of grief is that they deal with their grief in spurts, then

---

It has been a month since Dad died. Aaron is six years old and in the first grade. His sister, Kate, is ten years old and in the fourth grade.

Aaron is no longer doing well in school. His teach[er] complains that he cannot sit still and won't pay attention in class. At home he spends all his time arguing with Mom and Kate.

Kate complains that her stomach hurts all the tim[e]. She refuses to talk about her dad. Her grades are okay, but she no longer shows much interest in her friends.

Mom describes herself as a "nervous wreck." She fe[els] lonely, frightened, and overwhelmed; and she has fre[-]quent stomach problems and headaches. She is not sleeping well and has lost more than ten pounds.

Understanding How Children Grieve

Children react in dramatic and intensely painful ways to the death of a loved one, yet they may show their grief only intermittently. One reason fo[r] this is that children do not have the vocabulary necessary to express their grief. Even older childre[n] find it difficult to verbalize their painful and often confusing thoughts and feelings. A child is more likely to respond to grief by

▲ expressing fears for personal survival ("What is going to happen to me? What if something hap[-] pens to you?")
▲ demonstrating separation anxiety
▲ having problems with bedtime, school depar- ture, a parent's work departure
▲ exhibiting problems with social skills
▲ having difficulty making friends
▲ finding it difficult to trust new caregivers
▲ being angry, overactive, or aggressive
▲ expressing intense feelings such as sadness, guil[t] shame, pessimism, hopelessness, despair
▲ demonstrating control issues
▲ refusing to follow a normal plan for going to bed, doing homework, or eating
▲ slowing down in maturation, or even regressing in some behaviors
▲ losing self-esteem
▲ refusing to try new things or to take on new tasks at school

Perhaps the greatest factor influencing a child's ability to understand and cope with the loss of a loved one is age. It is helpful to consider some of the differences among age groups.

2

Ages 2–4

If a child has had a previous experience that helped him or her to understand the concept of death, then his or her ability to cope is significantly enhanced. Even preschool children realize that a dead goldfish no longer swims and a lifeless bird no longer flies. Until the age of five, however, children do not understand the finality of death. Questions such as "When is Daddy coming back?" indicate that a child considers the situation to be temporary or reversible. At this age, a child's distress can also result in an increased number of illnesses, such as colds and ear infections.

Ages 5–8

Children aged five to eight often see death as a separate creature, such as a monster or a demon. They understand the finality of death, but they may believe that death can be avoided, outrun, or out-smarted. Because a child this age has a developmental tendency to shut out his or her feelings and lacks the skills to deal with the intensity of those feelings, the child may use denial as a means of coping—which adults often perceive as a nonchalant or "so what?" attitude. Hyperactivity is another form of denial children use to avoid thinking about what has happened. Early in this age range, children may assume that all events occur in response to their personal behavior. A child may believe that the deceased has deliberately chosen to go away because the child was bad, and that if he or she acts "super good," the loved one will return.

Regression is also common for children this age. Previously self-directed children may have trouble being alone and may need constant playmates. Other children may begin to whine like preschoolers; cling to mementos, such as clothing, letters, and pictures; or have nightmares, high anxiety, or psychosomatic symptoms, such as tummy aches and exaggerated reactions to injuries. Adults are often impatient with a child's regression. The truth is that if a child is allowed to fall back to more familiar, simple ground until he or she can regain emotional balance, it is possible for the child to emerge stronger and more confident than before.

Age 9 and Up

Children aged nine and up see death as final and inevitable. They worry about their own survival and get back to "normal" for a time. They do as much as they can manage at any one time, then leave it. Enumerate the responses in this section and explain to parents that these are normal and predictable. Parents can help by anticipating these and reassuring their children when insecurities appear. Notice that many of these responses are similar to the reactions of children to divorce, which is a loss as well.

Differences by Age

These developmental differences are crucial to understanding how a child perceives death. Group parents together by the ages of their children, and let them work through the section that pertains to their children. Allow each group time to report to the whole class.

3

All Ages

Let the group as a whole discuss this section. Make a list of the adults in childrens' lives who should be told of the loss. (Teachers, Sunday school teachers, coaches, scout leaders, music teachers)

Suggested First Steps

Education

Discuss each of these points thoroughly. Encourage parents to let children ask questions. Sometimes they wonder about things parents would not think to address.

Reading together serves two purposes: it provides information and closeness. A grieving child needs large doses of both.

Permission

A child's grief is real and should be respected. Allowing the child to participate in the rituals of family mourning affirms that he is part of the family. It removes some of the uncertainty and mystery from what is happening. Remember that this may be the first time your child has seen you cry, and that will be frightening for her. If large crowds of friends or relatives are

that of other loved ones. Because they think concretely, they often misinterpret or misunderstand adults' comments, such as "You are the man of th house now," or "Be strong for your mother." Lik younger children, a child this age also may believe that the lost loved one left deliberately; but they will tend to blame the surviving parent for not pr venting it.

As a means of coping with guilt, anger, and depression, children of this age may distract them selves with equally intense involvement in sports, socializing (such as prolonged telephone conversa tions), or becoming absorbed in music (with head phones on to "tune out" everything and everyone Food can also become an important means of fin ing comfort, as the child confuses feelings of emp ness or loneliness with feelings of hunger.

All Ages

Children of all ages commonly experience diffic ties with learning and schoolwork after the loss of loved one. Parents and teachers need to recognize the persistent effect that grieving has on a child's learning, which can last well into the second year after the loved one's death. In addition to whatev tutorial help may be needed, patience and understanding will go a long way toward helping a chilc handle temporary learning difficulties.

Regardless of the difficulties children may exper ence after loss, all children need adults to help the grieve by understanding, acknowledging, and vali dating their experience.

Suggested First Steps
Education

Education simply means teaching children that major loss produces intense feelings that must be expressed. Letting children know that there are ca ing adults who want to talk about these feelings when the children are ready often gives them the permission and confidence they need to open up.

Family sharing, in particular, can be extremely effective. When the whole family talks together, a child learns not only about his or her own grief exp rience but also about those of other family member

Here are some suggestions:

▲ Select age-appropriate books you can read together. Include books about loss and books that help children understand their feelings.

4

Encourage everyone to share his or her thoughts and feelings. Tell a child that it will take some time before he or she feels better, but that these feelings will not last forever.

Make a point to explain that "nothing you thought or did caused Daddy (or Mommy or Grandmother) to die." Use clear language, saying that the person died rather than using the word *sleep* or the phrase *passed away*, which can be confusing or frightening to young children. Review practical adjustments that will affect a child's life, such as changes in routines, activities, and schedules.

Permission

Permission means that whenever a child tries to share his or her anger, guilt, sadness, or shame in verbal or physical ways, you do not ask the child to postpone, deny, or cover up these feelings. When a child opens up, stop whatever you are doing, get physically close, and try not to fall apart yourself. Use uncritical, matter-of-fact listening, without demonstrating shock or offering any kind of correction, but give yourself permission to show your sadness too.

Permission also means involving a child in rituals of family mourning, such as being present during family visitation, attending the funeral, visiting the cemetery, and offering spontaneous remembrances. Children over the age of four should be included in the funeral, or at least some part of it; however, the child will need a designated caregiver who is not intensely mourning and may leave with the child if he or she becomes overwhelmed at any time. Prepare the child well in advance for what he or she will see and hear at the funeral.

Support

Support is the continued presence, over time, of caring adults who are affectionate, honest, and emotionally available to a child for as long as needed. Grieving children need supportive relationships with both men and women. Older children can make these surrogate choices for themselves, but younger children need concerned adults to make provisions for them.

One of the most basic ways to provide support for a grieving child is to review each day's routine so that he or she knows what to expect. Anticipate and cope with separation anxiety by being reliable

5

around, be sure to allow some private time for yourself and your children.

Support

Support for a grieving child must be ongoing. The child will need extra care for a long time. The physical aspects of grieving are often overlooked; be sure to note them. Remember that children have friends, too. Their friends may not know what to do or say, but provide opportunities for them to be together. Your child will be ready to do normal things sooner than you will.

Symbols

A concreste object like a rock, a piece of jewelry or other memento can be a helpful centering tool for grieving children, giving place and substance to their feelings.

What to Do If This Isn't Working

There are times when extra help or another approach is needed. Summarize this list on the chalkboard or newsprint and discuss each.

▲ Help your child feel secure

▲ Be aware of anniversaries

▲ Talk about feelings

▲ Seek channels for expression

▲ Help child help him/herself

▲ Work with teachers

and predictable in your returns. Reassure a younger child by giving him or her a personal item for which the child knows you will return. An older child will benefit from having his or her own watch. Regardless of age, encourage the child to ask for whatever he or she needs (e.g., "I need an extra hug").

Because grieving is physically exhausting, the child's rest should be a priority. Plan for an earlier bedtime; and if separation anxiety is interfering with sleep, use soft, cuddly blankets (or perhaps an electric blanket) and a softly-playing bedside radio or tape player to make the bed warm and inviting.

Nourishment is another important consideration. Avoid control struggles over food by being flexible at mealtimes. During this difficult period, rely on the child's favorite foods supplemented with vitamins to provide basic nutritional needs.

If grieving interferes with parenting, extended family members and friends who are not as emotionally devastated by the loss are critically important to the child. Their remembrances of the deceased can help strengthen positive memories and build an understanding of who the loved one was, as well as how much the child was loved (e.g., "I remember how proud your mom was when..."). Children up to the age of twelve will need things such as pictures, scrapbooks, videos, and calendars to anchor and reinforce their own memories. If possible, every grieving child should have a picture of himself or herself with the deceased to help remind the child of their special relationship.

Support also means recognizing that children may postpone their grieving until it feels "safe." What constitutes "safe" for a child may include waiting until the surviving parent is functioning again, until home life settles down, or until there is another stable relationship that makes the child feel secure enough to express his or her feelings.

Finally, it is important to teach children that they will re-grieve losses as they mature. New experiences, such as the first time a child plays ball in the backyard without Dad, will cause the child to re-experience the reality of the loss.

What to Do If This Isn't Working

▲ Find as many ways as possible to help the child feel more secure.

▲ Anticipate and plan ahead for upcoming anniversaries, such as the child's and the deceased's birthdays and the day of the death.

6

Discuss basic feelings and use face drawings and/or mimicry to help the child identify and express each emotion. Bring out a child's angry feelings by playing games, such as the "It's not fair that–" game.

- Find physical ways for the child to express himself or herself, such as dancing, playing sports, or using clay or paints.
- Talk with the child about what he or she can do to reassure himself whenever necessary, such as repeating certain phrases in his or her mind or telling specific people that he or she needs help. Review with new teachers and other significant adults what has happened in the child's life, so that they too can be supportive.

When to Seek Help

Remember that all children have difficulties after the death of a loved one or another major loss, but some instances professional help may be needed

- if the child is consistently having problems, experiencing pain, or acting withdrawn (vs. periodic episodes);
- if symptoms get worse rather than better over time;
- if there is a sudden or dramatic change in the child's behavior;
- if a parent feels he or she cannot cope. (Note: Parents must have a way to take care of their own grieving before they can guide children in their grieving.)
- if there are extremes in the child's behavior, such as the absence of sadness, severe depression, continuous acting out, or overly responsible behavior.

A pastor or family ministries professional will be able to provide recommendations regarding therapists or counselors, support groups, and other sources for grieving children and families.

The Faith Perspective

Psalm 18:1-3, 6

I love you, O LORD, my strength.
The LORD is my rock, my fortress, and my deliverer,
my God, my rock in whom I take refuge,
my shield, and the horn of my salvation,
    my stronghold.
In my distress I called upon the LORD;
to my God I cried for help.
From his temple he heard my voice,
and my cry to him reached his ears.   (NRSV)

7

When to Seek Help

Since all children will have problems after the death of a loved one, it is important to be familiar with these guidelines that indicate more serious responses. A critical factor is whether or not the parent is coping well enough to evaluate his or her child. A grieving parent must have a support group--friends, relatives, anyone who can step in to encourage the parent to seek help when needed.

Closing

(2-3 minutes)
For centuries persons have turned to God for strength in the face of loss. The Psalms are the prayers and songs of Israel, and speak for all who grieve. Do not neglect your spiritual needs (or your child's) during this time. Be prepared to talk to your child about your beliefs about what happens after death. Answer his questions honestly. Seek help from your pastor if you need to clarify your own understandings.

Read Psalm 18:1-3, 6 as your closing prayer

Children in grief often need reassurance and sign of stability. Even though the physical presence of the family member is gone, the love and memories of the child will continue. Concrete symbols of the lasting love may be appealing, particularly to young children. Have the child select a symbol, such as a rock as in Psalm 18, that will remind the child not only of the family member but also of God's love and the love of the church community that will never go away. Have the child place the symbol in special location like the mantle or dinner table as a constant reminder.

Recommended Resources

For reading with children

Badger's Parting Gifts, by Susan Varley, (Mulberry books, 1992).

Lifetimes: The Beautiful Way to Explain Death to Children, by Bryan Mellonie (Bantam Books, 1987).

The Cherry Blossom Tree: A Grandfather Talks about Life an Death, by Jan Godfrey and Jane Cope (Augsburg, 1996)

Waterbugs and Dragonflies: Explaining Death to Young Children, by Doris Stickney (Pilgrim Press, 1997).

When Someone You Love Dies: An Explanation of Death for Children, by Robert V. Dodd (Abingdon Press, 1986).

For Adults

Helping Children Cope with the Loss of a Loved One: A Guide for Grownups, by William C. Kroen, Ph.D. (Free Spirit Publishing, 1996).

For more resources visit www.FaithHome.com.

About the Authors

Beth Sheller is a psychiatric clinical nurse specialist in private practice at Center for the Family in Nashville, Tennessee. She has worked with grieving children, individuals, and families for twenty years.

Gretchen B. Watts is a Jungian-oriented licensed clinical social worker in private practice. She is an associate member of Sandplay Therapists of America and has co-authored the book *The Friendly Classroom for a Small Planet: Children's Creative Response to Conflict*. Gretchen and her husband an daughter are members of St. George's Episcopal Church in Nashville, Tennessee.

FaithHome for Parents provides the church community with resources to support families and help children *to increase their faith confirm their hope, and perfect them in love.*

Your Child and Anger

How to Manage Anger and Resolve Conflict

FaithHome for Parents™

Gathering Time
(4-5 minutes)

Have paper and pencils available for class members. As persons arrive, ask them to write down two things that make them angry and two things that make their children angry. Ask for two volunteers to be prepared to do a short roleplaying exercise of an angry situation between two five year olds.

When everyone has arrived, do the roleplay.

Begin with this prayer or one of your own:
Dear God, Everybody feels anger sometimes, even you. Help us to express our anger appropriately and without being hurtful. Help us to teach our children to do the same, and to live in peace with one another, In the name of Jesus. Amen.

Scenario

(8-10 minutes)

Read the scenario from the booklet (the story printed in italics).

Say:

You know that your three-year-old can make you lose your patience sometimes. Imagine what he can do to another three year old! You at least are an adult, with adult perspective, vocabulary, and coping skills.

Ask:

Given the scene described in the story, what should Lacey's mother do?

The author makes a distinction between "responding" and "reacting" to situations. What do you think the difference is?

Angry actions often result in angry reactions, like a pendulum that swings wider and wider. In other words, anger escalates until someone makes a conscious decision to back away from it and make another response.

Anger has also been compared to a red hot ball which one person throws to another. The intended "receiver" of the ball gets burned if he catches it—if he accepts the anger and gets drawn into it. Instead,

Lacey is playing with her neighbor, Thomas, the downstairs playroom of her home when La spots Scruff, her favorite stuffed animal. She picks Scruff up and gives him a big hug. Suddenly, Thomas grabs Scruff away. "I want it!" he says as he holds the stuffed animal tight against his chest.

"It's mine!" says Lacey as she tries to pull Scruff away from Thomas.

"But I want to play with him!" yells Thoma pushing Lacey away.

Lacey falls backward over a toy truck. Furio she lunges toward Thomas and punches his ar The screaming continues, along with more hit kicks, hair pulling, and a scratch right below Thomas' left eye.

Suddenly Lacey's mom appears at the top of the stairs. "What is happening here?"

Lacey and Thomas could live in Anytown, USA. Most parents deal with similar circumstances regularly, and certainly all parents de with conflict and aggressive behavior at one time or another. How we parents handle the difficult situations may make a difference no only in the escalation of the conflict but also in the unnecessary perpetuation of violence.

Children and adults must learn the skills to respond to situations, rather than to react, if we are to prevent future violence. Even parents whose children show no obvious signs o aggressive or violent behavior cannot afford ignore the issue. We must become proactive teaching our children non-violent behavior i we are to end the escalation of violence in o homes, schools, workplaces, and communitie

The Sobering "Big Picture"

America received a wake up call in 1999 with dramatic acts of school violence directe against students by students. But we had got ten that same call countless times before—in other schools across the country, in workplaces, on playgrounds, on street corners, in apartment houses, and in single-family dwellings in the most exclusive parts of town Somehow, the recent events seemed to shock

2

s more—perhaps because of the extent of the
lanning, the magnitude of the hardware, and
1e ages of the victims and perpetrators. It is
et another story of young people
nequipped to handle their own confusing
motions. Tragically, it is part of an epidemic
1at knows no racial, cultural, or economic
oundaries—and one involving people who
re quick to anger and quick to resort to
hysical solutions that too often result in seri-
us injury or death.

Who is responsible? The truth is, we all are.
very adult who cares about existing in a safe
nd healthy community shares the responsibil-
y of teaching young people the skills to
esolve conflicts without resorting to violence.
t's easy to blame the violence of our youth
n TV, movies, video games, and the prolifer-
tion of guns on the street and in private
omes. It's harder to work actively to create a
ociety that actually chooses—and cherishes—
1e concept of non-violence. Our schools and
hurches certainly can help us work toward
nis goal, but the best and most effective place
o begin is at home.

aith Perspective

If we are to win the battle against violence,
·e must make a commitment to building
haracter in our children. Many experts
·elieve that starting early, when our children
re young, is the only hope for our future. We
1ust begin by instilling in our children posi-
·ve character morals—or rules of conduct
·ased on an understanding of right and
·rong. We can do this by encouraging—and
pholding as important, valuable, and expect-
d—ideals such as honesty, doing the "right"
hing, respecting self, respecting others, car-
1g, nurturing family and friends, and accept-
1g responsibility.

As Christians, we base this value system on
he life and character of Jesus. He not only
·aught us how to live; he showed us by his
xample. Of course, as parents, we are our
hildren's closest and most effective role mod-
·ls. Our children will follow our examples,

3

he can choose to step back
and let the ball of anger fall
to the ground, refusing to
play the other's game. This
is a concept that can be
taught to older children.

The Big Picture

(5-8 minutes)
The primary lesson we need
to learn today is that anger
is a natural feeling. Anger is
okay; what we have to work
on is what we do with our
anger.

The Sobering "Big Picture"
The author calls the recent
school violence a part of a
"Big Picture," an epidemic
of "young people
unequipped to handle their
own confusing emotions."

Ask:
Do you agree with that
assessment? Why? Who is
responsible? Who is going
to make it better?

The Faith Perspective

(10 minutes)
Jesus led by "precept [prin-
ciple] and example."
Ask:
▲ Do your teachings and
  your actions match up?
▲ Think of a time your
  child saw you react
  angrily at someone.
Write on a chalkboard or
newsprint as you discuss

this section the ideals parents should expect:
▲ honesty
▲ doing the "right" thing
▲ respecting self
▲ respecting others
▲ caring
▲ nurturing family and friends
▲ accepting responsibility

Discuss how living by these values will help children cope with anger.

Managing Anger and Resolving Conflict

(10 Minutes)
There are two steps listed in resolving angry situations:
▲ Step One: Identify the real cause of the anger.
▲ Step Two: Work with—not against—those involved to solve the problem.

Write on the chalkboard or newsprint as you discuss the steps toward resolution:
▲ Talk—words express feelings more effectively than physical violence
▲ Listen—to understand the other person's point of view to agree on what the problem is
▲ Compromise—get those involved to find a solution that everyone can accept

both good and bad. This is why it is so important that we live as Christ taught us to live so that in following us, our children will be helped to follow Christ. This may be one of the ways of role modeling Paul spoke of the Corinthians when he said, "Follow my example, as I follow the example of Christ" *Corinthians 11:1 NIV).*

The Sermon on the Mount, *Matthew 5-7,* offers a guide for living. Familiarize yourself with these three chapters and teach their instructions to your children by your example as well as by your words. It is important to remember that although we cannot live up to such high standards by our own power, we can become the people God desires us to be when we allow God to work in us.

Managing Anger and Resolving Conflict

Remember Lacey and Thomas from the opening story? Common occurrences of conflict in the home such as this serve as teachable moments—as catalysts for discussing and demonstrating peaceful ways to manage anger and resolve conflict. An important first step is to teach our children to identify the real cause of their anger or difficulty and then to work with—not against—those involved to solve the problem. Here are some helpful steps to try:
Talk.

When your child is demonstrating anger or aggressive behavior, talk with your child about the emotions he or she is feeling and ask questions to discover what has prompted those feelings.

Help your child name the problem and direct his or her words toward the circumstance rather than toward a person or group. With younger children, try this reminder: "Use your words." This oft-used phrase, spoken like a mantra at daycares and preschools, is helpful following an incident between two children that involves whining, screaming, pushing, or hitting. It is a reminder that words can express feelings more effectively, and with fewer negative consequences, than verbal or physical violence.

4

Encourage your child to use "I" rather than "you" language. ("I feel sad when you say mean things to me," rather than "You hurt my feelings.")

If your child resorts to blaming or name-calling, direct him or her to stick with the "issue."

Listen.

Actively listen to your child so that you understand his or her point of view.

Encourage your child to listen to the other person or persons involved in order to understand their points of view. To help a younger child understand how another person feels, ask questions that "turn the tables," such as, "How would you feel if someone took your favorite stuffed animal from you?"

Agree.

Direct your child and the others involved to come to an agreement on the nature of the problem. With younger children, you will need to assist in this process.

If children, particularly older children, cannot agree on the problem, help each articulate his or her own viewpoint. After listening to each child, paraphrase the problem as each perceives it, asking for agreement from the children on your restatement of the problem.

Compromise.

Encourage your child and those involved to work together to find a solution that everyone can live with.

If necessary, turn to a mediator or a third party with an objective perspective.

Ultimately, children need to understand that it is okay to feel angry, but it's not okay to channel that anger in ways that physically or verbally hurt other people.

Activities for Teaching Non-violence

▲ Monitor your child's TV viewing. It's hard to avoid violence on TV, and it's hard to keep kids from watching it. The average child has seen 100,000 violent acts on TV by the end of sixth grade. (*Parents Magazine*, June 1999, from "Should TV news be Rated R?") But with proper super-

5

Activities for Teaching Non-violence
(5 minutes)

▲ Monitor your child's TV consumption.

▲ Note that some children are more impressionable than others. Age may not be the only indicator of what is permissible for a child to watch.

▲ Read together the stories of heroes of non-violence.

▲ Discuss with your child how these leaders made a difference. How would their stories be different if they had used force?

▲ Involve your child in service projects. A child who feels empowered to change things, to make a difference, will learn new ways to attack problems.

When and Where to Seek Help

It is important to notice that some of the warning signs listed here do not appear to involve anger, for example, lack of interest in school or withdrawal from family and friends. However, some psychologists define depression as "anger turned inward." Emphasize to the class that the warning signs are cumulative—the more signs you see, the higher the risk. On the other hand, do not ignore a problem simply because it is the only one.

vision, you can decrease the amount of violence your child is exposed to on TV by creating a list of programs that are inappropriate or "off limits." Then make a commitment to watch any questionable shows with your child, taking advantage of any educational opportunities that may arise. Here are a few suggestions for some possible family discussions:

◆ What conflict or situation was presented in the show?
◆ What are some alternative non-violent solutions to the same problem or circumstance?
◆ What might have been the real-life consequences for each of the parties involved?

Remember, your own TV viewing habits speak volumes to your child.

▲ Your child can learn valuable insights about practicing non-violence from the stories of famous peace promoters such as Mahatma Gandhi, Martin Luther King, Jr., Menachem Begin, and Anwar el-Sadat. Choose those world leaders you and your child would enjoy reading about and discussing together.
▲ Involve your child in church and community service projects. Through outreach, children begin to recognize their own abilities to make a positive difference in the world while learning to respect others who may be different from themselves.

When and Where to Seek Help

Repeated incidents of school violence in recent years have caused us to have heightened sensibilities about our children's behaviors, as well as the observed actions of their peers. It is sometimes difficult to differentiate between "normal" acting out and conduct that crosses the line. Experts point to the following "warning signs":

▲ lack of interest in school
▲ persistent disregard for rules or authority
▲ cruelty to pets or other animals
▲ constant talk about violence or weapons
▲ fixation with violent games, movies, and TV shows

6

- gang involvement
- withdrawal from family and friends
- artwork or writing that presents themes of violence, anger, or isolation
- bringing, or even talking about bringing, a weapon to school
- frequent loss of temper or extreme irritability

The more of these signs that are evident, the higher the risk—and the greater the need for taking immediate action. A valuable source of information is your child's teacher(s), who may have helpful insights related to your child's behavior, school performance, peer group, and any areas or issues of concern. The school's guidance counselor and your church community can provide helpful information and support. Check with your pastor to learn about counseling services your church may offer or recommend or find a family therapist in your area by visiting www.aamft.org.

A Prayer of Peace

We all encounter events during the course of our busy days that "push our buttons" or simply test our commitment to act peacefully toward others. In those moments, remember that you can find solace in prayer. Here is a prayer that may serve as a daily reminder of our peaceful purpose:

Lord, make me an instrument of your peace.
Where there is hatred, let me sow love.
Where there is injury, pardon.
Where there is doubt, faith.
Where there is despair, hope.
Where there is darkness, light.
Where there is sadness, joy.
Divine Master,
Grant that I may not so much seek
To be consoled as to console,
To be understood as to understand,
To be loved as to love,
For it is in giving that we receive,
It is in pardoning that we are pardoned,
It is in dying that we are born to eternal life.
—St. Francis of Assisi, 1181-1226

Your Assignment
(2-3 minutes)
Ask the class to take time this week to read the Sermon on the Mount (Matthew 5-7) in a modern translation.

Say:
Consider how living by Jesus' standards will lead to a healthy, peaceful life. Consider how it will cause you to be out of step with the world. Consider how such a life lived by Christians everywhere could change the world. Pray that God's grace will help you live such a life.

Closing
(1-2 minutes)
Close by reading in unison the Prayer of St. Francis of Assisi, found on page 7 of the booklet.

Recommended Resources

Tired of Yelling: Teaching Our Children to Resolve Conflict, by Lyndon D. Waugh (Longstreet, Inc., 1999).

For Children

Andrew's Angry Words, by Dorothea Lachner (North-South, 1997). Ages 5-8

Let's Talk About Feeling Angry, by Joy Berry (Scholastic, Inc., 1995). Ages 2-6

When I'm Angry, by Jane Aaron (Golden Books, 1998). Ages 3-6

For more resources visit www.FaithHome.com

About the Authors

Ned Andrew Solomon is a part-time freelance writer. He lives in Nashville with his wife Amy, and two daughters, Skye and Lizzy B. He has written articles on family issues for *Nashville Life*, FamilyZone, KidZone, and *Parents Magazine*. He is the author of Project Solution, The Tennessean's character education newspaper for children in Nashville's Metro Schools. His full-time job is conducting research with children who have language delays and behavior difficulties at the Peabody College of Vanderbilt University.

Sally Sharpe, series editor for FaithParent, lives with her husband, Neil, and their two young daughters in Mt. Juliet, Tennessee. She has been an editor for thirteen years, with eight of those years devoted to Abingdon Press and Dimensions for Living books. As well as editing, Sally wrote "The Faith Perspective" section of Your Child and Anger.

The Scripture quotations noted NIV are taken from the Holy Bible: New International Version, Copyright © 1973, 1978, 1984 by the International Bible Society. Used by permission of Zondervan Bible Publishers. All rights reserved.

FaithHome for Parents provides the church community with resources to support families and help children *to increase their faith, confirm their hope, and perfect them in love.*

ISBN 068703401-9

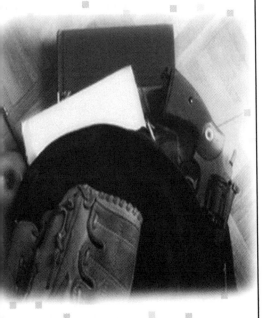

Your Child and Violence

Talking to Your Child in the Aftermath

FaithHome for Parents ™

Gathering Time
(8-10 minutes)

Have index cards and pens available.

Copy on a chalkboard or newsprint the words of Isaiah 43:1b-3a (NRSV):

Do not fear for I have redeemed you; I have called you by name, you are mine. When you pass through the waters, I will be with you; and through the rivers, they shall not overwhelm you; when you walk through fire you shall not be burned, and the flame shall not consume you. For I am the Lord your God, the Holy One of Israel, your Savior.

As class members arrive, invite them to write the words on a card to give to their child. The child may want to tape it to the bathroom mirror, where she will see it every morning, or in a plastic sleeve in the notebook she carries to school.

Prayer
Begin with this prayer or one of your own:

God of all promises, thank you for understanding our fears, and how helpless they can make us feel. Our hearts ache when we hear of violent acts, of persons who are hurt, of life destroyed. Give us courage to be part of the solution. Help us to protect our children and all children. And grant us peace, in the name of the Prince of Peace. Amen.

Scenario

(3-4 minutes)
Read the scenario from the booklet (the story printed in italics).

Say:
Kayla's question—How will you stop them?—is a question that all parents must have asked themselves in the aftermath of recent school violence. Kayla's concern is our concern: in the face of random and unpredictable violence, how will we protect our children? This lesson will help us answer Kayla's question.

Talk About It

(5 minutes)
Adults understand risk: life is risky, riding in a car is risky, eating food in a restaurant is risky. But we can understand the odds, and know that chances are, things will be okay. When a child learns that terrible things can happen, they do not have the maturity to manage their anxiety.

Sandy grabbed her travel coffee mug and picked up her car keys from the kitchen counter. "C'mon, sweet girl!" she called at the bottom of the stairs. "Time for school." She waited a few seconds and then climbed the steps to her six-year-old daughter's room. There was Kayla, sitting on the floor in the corner, her legs pulled in close to her chest. Sandy could see that Kayla's eyes were full of tears.

"What's the matter, Kay?" Sandy asked, kneeling on the floor next to her.

"Not going," said Kayla. "Not going back EVER."

"Why, honey?" asked Sandy, running her fingers through her daughter's long, brown hair.

"Because there are bad people with guns," said Kayla, her voice shaky. "And when we lay on our mats for quiet time, they could kill me and my friends. You said so yourself!"

Suddenly, Sandy remembered her phone conversation with her best friend, Linda. They were discussing how frightened they were after the recent school shootings. Kayla had been playing with her bean bag toys in the next room.

"Oh, honey," Sandy said, holding Kayla close. "Mommy won't let that happen."

Kayla looked up, her eyes red from crying. "But how will you stop them?"

The tragic events in schools across the country where violence has erupted have left both children and adults with feelings of sadness, fear, anxiety, and confusion. The question arises in almost every news story about school violence: Can the same type of thing happen here? Unfortunately, the answer is yes; violent tragedies can and do happen anywhere.

We all are affected by seemingly senseless acts of violence. They actually alter the way we live our lives, where we go, and what we do when we get there. Understandably, many parents—especially those with young children—are afraid to let their kids out of their sight for even a second.

There's no doubt about it: We live in an extremely violent world. News reports are filled with stories of murder and mayhem, relayed in gruesome detail. TV shows, movies, and videos are rampant with killings and beatings. Violent

2

video games get more vivid, intense, and popular each year. It's no wonder so many kids grow up believing that the "bad people" are around every corner, and that the only ways to handle conflict are violent ones.

So how can we help our children feel safe in this environment, especially after they have been affected—whether directly or indirectly—by a violent incident? First and foremost, we must talk with our children. We all know that ignoring an unpleasant incident will not make it go away, yet sometimes it is easier to remain silent. Remember, however, that your silence actually may contribute to your child's feelings of anxiety and insecurity.

Talk About It

Here are a few suggestions for opening the lines of communication with your child:

▲ Never assume your child is unaware of what has happened. Kids pick up everything, especially your reactions.

▲ Realize that you can talk honestly about a violent incident without going into unnecessary graphic detail.

▲ Share your own feelings about the situation. It may help your child to know that you are afraid sometimes, too.

▲ Answer your child's questions as honestly and completely as you can.

▲ Encourage your child to talk about his or her concerns and feelings—in general, as well as in response to a particular incident.

▲ If your child is hesitant to discuss an incident, ask what he or she has heard about it and how this makes him or her feel.

▲ Never minimize your child's anxieties or fears. Avoid making statements such as, "There's nothing to be afraid of." Remember that your child's fear is very real.

Reassure Your Child

Listening to and acknowledging your child's fears is an important first step in reassuring your child. Here are some other effective ways to meet your child's need for reassurance:

▲ Reaffirm all the ways you and your family, your child's teachers, and others work to keep your child safe. Talk through specifics, includ-

It is important to talk to your child about violent incidents they see or hear of. They will feel relieved to be able to talk, and not to have to keep their feelings secret.

Discuss briefly each of the hints on how to talk to your child. Never minimize or say Don't be silly. By doing that, you have left the child with his fears and added another—now he is afraid he doesn't know what he should fear.

Reassure Your Child

(10 minutes)
The booklet says that the media and popular culture would have us believe that bad people are around every corner.
Ask:
▲ Do you believe there are bad people?
▲ Do you believe there are good people?

Talk with your child about those good people, all the good people they encounter every day and who help keep them safe: parents, teachers, crossing guards, policemen, doctors, friends. Tell your child that there are good people every-where, even though all peo-

3

ple are not necessarily good. If your child has particular concerns at school or in the neighborhood, allow him to choose one adult he feels comfortable with to be his special friend, someone to tell if he has difficulty. An ally can be a powerful source of comfort. With multiple incidents of school violence, teachers and parents (as well as our children!) are more aware of the potential dangers and are more vigilant and observant. Teachers and school administrators are quick to act on threats or suspicious behavior.

Limit and Supervise Media Exposure

(5 minutes)
Key words here: limit and supervise. It takes work and time, but it is important enough to warrant the effort.

Ask:
What kinds of limits do you have on TV and movies?
Do you differ these by age?
How do you think your presence with your child expands or effects what you watch?

ing the way you secure your house or apartment, how you arrange your child's time away from you, any neighborhood watch or community effort, and school safety plans.
▲ Let your child talk through what he or she would do in case of a crisis at school or home—even if some of your child's fears seem extreme. Children sometimes need to "talk it through" several times to reassure themselves.
▲ Visit or be as visible as you can in the arena where your child is most afraid, whether it is at school, at a neighborhood playground, or somewhere else.
▲ Teach your child age-appropriate ways to call for help, to be safe, and to practice self-defense. Include the basics for a younger child, such as knowing his or her last name, home address, and phone number; your name and where you work; and how to dial 911. The National Crime Prevention Council (www.ncpc.org) and The Polly Klaas Foundation (www.pollyklaas.org) offer helpful information to parents on child safety.

Limit and Supervise Media Exposure

Perhaps one of the most important measures you can take to help your child cope with his or her fears related to violence is to limit and supervise your child's exposure to the media, especially TV news reports. Many experts believe that although news programming is educational, most young children and many older children cannot handle or process in a healthy way the frightening images presented in news broadcasts. Research has further shown that the younger the child is, the longer the negative effects last. It doesn't help matters that some of the most sensational news stories are the ones that involve violence to children.

Of course, with the exception of very young children, it is impossible to shelter children from all media coverage of violent events; and with older children, it is unwise to try to do so. The key words to remember are *limit* and *supervise*. The younger the child, the more you will want to limit or eliminate exposure. Whatever your child's age, watch news reports

4

together and discuss what you have seen and heard as well as how you feel about it.

Help to Create Safe Environments

Beyond talking with your child, what can you do to keep your child safe from violence? There are no short-term answers. Many of the most tragic events reported in the news appear to be random and hard to predict. For long-term change, you can work with your church, community, and family to create safer places.

Creating a safer home. Practicing some basic safety measures will help your child— and yourself—feel better about safety. You will want to give some careful thought to the safety measures that will make your home a safer place. Here are a couple of examples to help you get started:

▲ Monitor your child's use of the internet. This not only protects your child from age-inappropriate and frightening sites, but it also helps to keep your child safer from internet predators who want to contact youngsters. Make sure that your child knows never to reveal any personal information—even name and age—to strangers on the Net.

▲ Make gun safety an important issue in your home. Thirteen children die each day in the U.S. from gunshot wounds; four times as many are wounded. Many of these incidents are not the result of violence in schools or neighborhoods; rather, they are self-inflicted acts or accidents resulting from access to guns in the home. If you choose to have a gun in your home, practice and teach stringent gun safety. Whether you own firearms or not, talk to your child about guns and gun safety. Know about the households your child visits and talk to the parents about their views on firearms.

Creating a safer church. A church forms a safe haven for families. There are precautions that any congregation can take to assure the highest level of safety for children. For help, see *Safe Sanctuaries*, featured in the Recommended Resources section.

Creating safer schools. The National PTA suggests a number of ways that parents can

5

Help to Create Safe Environments
(10 minutes)

▲ Let your child know the safety measures you take in your home—locks, smoke alarms, fire extinguishers, lights.

▲ Monitor use of internet at home.

▲ Make sure safety precautions imortant to you (TV, internet, gun safety, unsupervised time outdoors) are practiced at all friends' homes.

▲ Work with your church and school leaders to create safer environments.

When and Where to Turn for Help

Emphasize that seeking help when it is needed is the responsible thing to do. It is not over-reacting. If your child worries incessantly without improvement, seek outside help. Parents also may want more individual help dealing with their own or their child's fears.

Warning Signs Indicating a Tendency for Violence

The warning signs are particularly important. Know what the danger signs are and be alert for them. By so doing, you will protect your own child and possibly many others.

work with teachers and administrators to create safer schools. Their website (www.pta.org) and a special site on children and violence (www.pta.org/events/violprev) offer a wealth of good information.

The Department of Education, the National PTA, and seventeen other education and mental health associations issued a report in 1998 titled "Early Warning, Timely Response." This report outlines characteristics of a safe school and offers help for setting up crisis intervention, getting help for troubled children and creating prevention plans and emergency plans. (www.ed.gov/offices/OSERS/OSEP/early-wrn.html)

When and Where to Turn for Help

With patience and open communication, you and your child should be able to work through your fears and concerns together. If, however, you are worried about your child's reaction or have ongoing concerns about his or her behavior or emotions, seek help from other resources: a teacher who is familiar with your child, a guidance counselor, a pastor or Christian counselor, a psychologist, or a crisis hot line. An outside perspective often can provide a beneficial alternative.

To easily find a certified family therapist in your area, try the online directory at www.aamft.org or ask your pastor, the school counselor or local mental health associate for a resource list.

Warning Signs Indicating a Tendency for Violence

Though there is no way to consistently predict violence, psychologists have developed lists of behaviors that may indicate a tendency for violence in children of all ages. Individually, many of the behaviors are not problems. Children with violent tendencies usually exhibit several of these signs, showing the signs frequently and at an increasing intensity over time. If you observe these behaviors repeatedly in your child or in his or her classmates, seek help from a Christian counselor, your child's school, or a family therapist.

6

Very Young Children
▲ Engages in play with violent themes
▲ Is cruel to other children
▲ Seems unusually detached from parents
▲ Multiple temper tantrums and aggressive outbursts in single day

School-Age Children
▲ Cruel toward pets or other animals
▲ Patterns of impulsive hitting; tries to control others through violence
▲ Difficulty accepting criticism or teasing; reacts with rage or blame
▲ Poor academic performance; difficulty participating in the classroom
▲ Drawn to violence in TV, movies, video games
▲ Has trouble making and keeping friends due to his or her behavior
▲ Overly violent drawings, writing, or poetry if the violence depicted is toward a specific individual or group
▲ Reflects intense prejudices and intolerance toward others based on race, ability, appearance, or sexual orientation

Teens
▲ Consistently insensitive to the feelings of others
▲ Relies on physical violence to get what he or she wants
▲ Expresses feelings of persecution and isolation often
▲ Poor academic performance; often skips school or drops out
▲ Substance abuse
▲ Involved in crimes that show disrespect of authority and property

Faith Perspective
In the aftermath of violence, it is natural to question God and even to be angry at God. Yet God understands our hurt, our pain, our confusion, and our fear. Though at times we may feel alone or abandoned, the truth is that God is always with us and will never desert us.

It is especially important for children to know that God watches over them and is with them wherever they go. Here are a few

7

Closing
Encourage parents to help children memorize one or more of the Scriptures listed in this section. Parents may want to give a child something tangible to remind them that God is always near--a pocket cross, or a small polished rock.

Assignment
(4-5 minutes)
Perhaps you (or the class as a whole) would like to explore the Internet (several websites are listed in the booklet) and find a way to get involved in an effort to make your community safer.

Prayer
O God,
Draw us near to you. Shelter us under your wing, like a mother hen. Keep us in your love for Christ's sake. Amen

Scriptures you may want to share with your child

Psalm 23:4   *Psalm 91:11-13, 15*
Matthew 10:29-31   *Romans 8:35-39*

The Bible also assures us that God is greater than our fears. God not only comforts us; God gives us the strength to conquer our fears:

Psalm 27:1   *Psalm 46*
John 14:27   *John 16:33*

During times of fear and anxiety, remember that prayer can bring comfort and peace—a peace that surpasses all understanding (Philippians 4:7) Pray for your child and with your child, never doubting that God both hears and answers prayer.

Recommended Resources:

Mommy, I'm Scared: How TV and Movies Frighte Children and What We Can Do to Protect Them, by Joanne Cantor (Harvest Books, 1998).

Safe Sanctuaries: Reducing the Risk of Child Abuse in the Church, by Joy Thornburg Melto (Discipleship Resources, 1998).

For Older Children (10-14)

The Safe Zone, by Donna Chaiet and Francine Russell (Morrow Junior Books, 1998)

For more resources visit www.FaithHome.com.

About the Author

Ned Andrew Solomon is a part-time free-lance writer. He lives in Nashville with his wife, Amy, and two daughters, Skye and Lizzy B. He has written articles on family issues for *Nashville Life* FamilyZone, KidZone and *Parents Magazine*. He is the author of Project: Solution, The Tennessean's character education newspaper for children in Nashville's Metro Schools. His full-time job is conducting research with children who have language delays and behavior difficulties at the Peabody College of Vanderbilt University.

FaithHome for Parents provides the church community with resources to *support families and help children to increase their faith, confirm their hope, and perfect them in love.*

ISBN 068703404-3

Parenting as Partners

Teamwork is an essential part of parenting.

Gathering Time
(8-10 Minutes)

As class members arrive invite them to sit down as couples (or with a partner if a spouse is not present) and talk about times when they have disagreed with their spouse over child-raising. These may be minor or serious differences of opinion, but encourage persons to be honest about themselves.

After they have exchanged stories, ask them to categorize their individual parenting style: relaxed, structured, reactionary, stern, strict, permissive, and so on. Then ask them to categorize their spouse's style.

Prayer

Open with this prayer or one of your own.

Dear Lord, We know how important parenting is, but sometimes we feel unequal to the task. Help us to help each other, and help us to allow room for you in our marriage, in our family, in our home, in the name of the Christ. Amen.

Scenario

Read the scenario from the booklet (the story printed in italics).

Ask:

What would you say to Jack?

What would you say to Marcy?

Say:

The story is told about a couple who were in a heated argument. Finally the wife held up her left hand and pointed to her wedding ring. "Hey, remember I'm on your side!" she said. This session will help us to remember that.

For those of you who do not have a spouse, think about who is playing on your "team." Who is available to help you with tough decisions and the workload of being a parent?

Philosophies of Parenting

(5 minutes)

Ask:

When did you first talk about parenting philosophies?

Before marriage? Before the birth of the firstborn? When the first disagreement arose? Today?

The list of topics for discussion is helpful. Even if you talked about this years ago,

"Maybe we weren't meant to be parents," Jack mused aloud as he and a coworker walked to lunch. "Perhaps we had the kids too close together—the twins are five now, and Jamie is two. All I know is that the responsibilities seem overwhelming, and our marriage is suffering. Marcy is consumed by the kids and has little time for me. And it seems we disagree about almost everything having to do with being a parent—from the best way to discipline the children to what kinds of birthday parties they should have."

Parenting is a rich but demanding calling. However, as Jack and Marcy discovered, the richness can be elusive and the demands staggering if parents are battling each other. For parenting to be a rich experience, you and your mate must view yourselves as a team. Following are some important principles for an effective parenting team.

Discuss your Experiences and Philosophies of Parenting

Ideally, you should discuss these matters before your children arrive, but it's never too late to begin. When you explore your individual philosophies and experiences, you gain a better understanding of each other's parenting preferences. You also identify possible problem areas. Here are some topics you'll want to discuss together:

▲ the kind of family life you hope to have (e.g., What's a good balance between separate and shared activities? Will Mom and Dad make all major decisions? Or, when the children are old enough, will you have regular family meetings which involve the children in decision-making?)

▲ the goals you will have for your children at various stages of their lives

▲ your parents' mode(s) of discipline and the extent you plan to use the same techniques

▲ your fondest childhood memories and

2

how you can help your children have similar experiences

▲ painful experiences with your parents that you want to avoid with your children

▲ the kinds of rules and responsibilities that you believe children need

Capitalize on Your Individual Strengths

One of the helpful things about being on a team is that each member contributes unique strengths that increase the team's effectiveness. Identify the strengths you each bring to parenting and discuss ways to make the most of them. For example, one of you may be a better listener when your child wants to talk about a problem. One of you may have more discretionary time to take your child to the doctor's office or to a birthday party. One of you may be more skilled at explaining questions of faith.

The list could go on. The point is this: Each of you has special strengths to contribute as a parent. Make the most of these strengths, but stay flexible because your contributions may change as your children grow. It's important to be sensitive to their needs. For instance, the child who mainly took his troubles to Mom when he was a toddler may be more comfortable discussing an adolescent problem with Dad.

Present a United Front on Important Matters

You probably will disagree at times about your roles as parents. You may disagree about matters of discipline, how much to spend on birthdays or Christmas, or rules and responsibilities for the children. Despite these differences, work out any disagreements behind the scenes and present a united front before your children. Children quickly learn to get what they want by playing one parent against the other. A united front lets them know it won't work.

3

you have grown and changed as parents. Perhaps it is time to revisit these questions. Try to find a time with few interruptions and when you are rested to have this parenting conference.

Capitalize on Your Individual Strengths

(5-8 minutes)
Give the class three or four minutes to talk with their partners about their individual strengths. Encourage them to be objective.

Try questions in your pairs like:
What responsibilities do you usually handle with your child?
Which do you feel you do well?
Which would you like to do well with help?
What kinds of things does your spouse or other family handle with greater ease?

Remind the class that there are times when one parent is tired or stressed or so close to a situation that he or she becomes ineffective. The other parent can step in and provide an alternative. (In team play, it's called "putting in a substitute.") Be sure the substitute doesn't just take over.

He or she needs to ask, "Would you like to take a break? I'll be glad to help here." That prevents the child from interpreting the switch as implying that one parent is inadequate.

Present a United Front on Important Matters
(5 Minutes)
Write these three headings on a chalkboard or newsprint as you discuss them.

▲ Discipline: Remember that it is okay to say "Your father and I will talk this over and get back to you," particularly if your children are older and if you have a tendency to differ on appropriate consequences.

▲ Family Time and Traditions: It takes time and work to build a solid, close family. Doing things together makes memories and traditions that will last forever.

▲ Religious Training: If at all possible, share involvement in worship and church activities.

In addition, children whose parents openly disagree on important matters may become confused or indecisive and be apt to dismiss the issues as unimportant.

Consider these three areas where you need a united front:

1. Discipline
Even young children recognize when parents are not a team—when, for instance, one parent is more permissive than the other. Invariably, they will use this information to set parent against parent and escape discipline. Being a team on discipline means…

▲ rules and boundaries are agreed upon and enforced by both parents.

▲ both parents take responsibility for teaching their children these rules and the consequences of breaking them.

▲ children understand that consequences are a joint decision and are consistently dispensed.

2. Family Time and Traditions
A spouse can undermine the team by not fully supporting family time and traditions. If, for example, Mom tells her reluctant children that they will attend the traditional annual family reunion, then Dad must not subvert the effort—even by a roll of the eyes. Often children fully appreciate such traditions only when they are grown. If one parent expresses reservations or reluctance, this appreciation may never develop.

The family time and traditions you should champion include…

▲ celebrating birthdays and holidays

▲ taking family vacations (even if your "vacation" means staying home and spending time together)

▲ eating dinner together regularly (each day if possible)

▲ having regular family discussions about the highlights, problems, and issues that face each family member (encourage the

4

discussion of feelings as well as events)
▲ sharing responsibilities for household chores
▲ attending together special events such as confirmation, graduation, and performances by a family member

3. Religious Training

One parent may be more skilled at teaching matters of faith, but both parents need to be committed to worship attendance and church activities. Parents who drop off their children at church are teaching them that religion is a childish affair and that faith isn't very important. But when Dad and Mom work together as a team to demonstrate the importance of faith, the children are more likely to make their own commitment to God.

Take Action to Keep Your Team Strong
1. Work Together to Deal with the Challenge of "Busy-ness"

Some parents fall into a competition for the dubious honor of "I'm busier than you are." If that's true, you're not working as a team. Face the fact: Caring for children is demanding and will keep you both busy. The challenge is to meet the demands of the task in a way that doesn't deplete you physically or emotionally.

Parenting partners can cope with the challenge of busy-ness by…
▲ sharing the work load so that you have similar amounts of leisure time
▲ being flexible, willing to take on additional tasks when your spouse is feeling overwhelmed, weary, or stressed
▲ assigning the children household tasks (appropriate to age and ability)
▲ limiting the number of activities in which your children participate
▲ setting priorities and saying "no" when demands and opportunities pile up

Take Action to Keep Your Team Strong

If you are in a small group of 8 or fewer, try this next section together. If you have more parents, split into smaller groups. With groups, assign each either one or two of the four topics.

Say:

It takes work and planning to keep your parenting partnership strong. We'll look at four issues: working together to handle busyness, nurturing your marriage, nurturing your faith, and staying a team.

Ask each group to brainstorm the issues and suggestions listed and add new ideas. Ask the groups to prioritize which tasks are not critical.

1. Work together. Raising children is hard work, but it doesn't last forever. Share the load and support each other.

2. Nurture your marriage. Your relationship is the foundation of the family. Keep it strong so that you can provide love and nurturing for your children.

3. Nurture your faith. Honor Christ in your

lives and in your home. Grow in faith together. Include God in your partnership.

4. Remain a parenting team whatever the circumstances. When times are hard, it will be difficult to function as a team, and yet that is the very time you absolutely must find a way to do it. If necessary, get professional help.

2. Nurture Your Marriage

You are husband and wife as well as father and mother. The stronger your marriage, the stronger you are as parents. So keep your marriage alive and meaningful:

▲ Spend some time together–just the two of you—each day.
▲ Keep courting one another.
▲ Express affection lavishly.
▲ Regularly affirm each other.
▲ Attend a marriage enrichment class, or read a book on building a vital marriage and discuss how you can implement its suggestions.

3. Nurture Your Faith

A strong faith strengthens your marriage and your parenting. Being a parenting team dramatically reduces the strain on each partner. Being a faith-based parenting team brings the power of God to the task.

An important way to nurture your faith is to engage in spiritual activities with your children. When you do this, you also nourish their faith and make your family a faith-based community. For example, attend worship together, say grace before meals and pray together at other times, read the Bible together, discuss spiritual issues and questions, and talk about how faith bears upon the demands of everyday life.

4. Remain a Parenting Team Whatever the Circumstances

Some situations—such as financial troubles, serious illness, and divorce—can severely test your commitment as parenting partners. For example, divorce often makes cooperation between parents a difficult task—even more so when there is a remarriage and stepfamily. Yet there are steps you can take as divorced parents to be effective parenting partners:

▲ Maintain your commitment to your children's well-being.

6

- ▲ Respect your ex-spouse as the parent of your children and don't undercut his or her role in their lives by using unkind or angry words.
- ▲ Don't argue about such things as visitation schedules or financial arrangements in front of your children.
- ▲ Communicate with each other on a regular basis about issues affecting your children. If "in person" communication is difficult, use e-mail or voice mail.

More and more parents in difficult situations are learning that they can, by the grace of God, rise above personal distress and marital disruption and continue to work together to nurture their children. It requires regular prayer, perhaps counseling, and a relentless focus on your children's needs and welfare. But you can do it. And when your children are grown, you will be deeply grateful that you did.

The Faith Perspective
Deuteronomy 7:12-13a
If you heed these ordinances by diligently observing them, the Lord your God will...love you, bless you, and multiply you; he will bless the fruit of your womb. (NRSV)

Matthew 19:14
But Jesus said, "Let the little children come to me, and do not stop them, for it is to such as these that the kingdom of heaven belongs." (NRSV)

Children are beloved of God. They are God's blessing to husbands and wives, who are called to be parenting partners. And the God who blesses you with children is the One "who by the power at work within us is able to accomplish abundantly far more than all we can ask or imagine" (Ephesians 3:20 NRSV). This promise means that God is also your partner and will enable you to fulfill your calling and reap the joy of being central figures in a holy task.

7

The Faith Perspective
(5 minutes)
Parents are partners in God's creative powers, and parenting is a holy task. Being a parent also teaches us about God and how patiently, unconditionally, and parentally he loves us.

Your Assignment
Find thirty minutes this week to talk about your family. Talk about your marriage, your children, how you're doing. Set a goal—give yourselves an assignment—something you would like to work on over the next month. Then follow through.

Closing
Close with this prayer or one of your own:
Dear God,
We thank You that we are not alone. You are with us and You have given us partners to share the load. Help us to work together for the sake of our children, the joy of our family, and the glory of your kingdom, in Jesus' name. Amen.

Recommended Resources

Becoming Family: How to Build a Stepfamily that Really Works by Robert H. Lauer and Jeanette C. Lauer (Augsburg, 1999).

How To Talk To Your Kids About Really Important Things by Charles E. Schaefer and Theresa Foy DiGeronimo (Jossey-Bass, 1994).

Perfect Parenting: The Dictionary of 1000 Parenting Tips by Elizabeth Pantley and William Sears (Contemporary Books, 1998).

**For more resources visit
www.FaithHome.com.**

About the Authors

Robert H. Lauer, Ph.D., and Jeanette C. Lauer, Ph.D., have co-authored fifteen books and numerous articles and have lectured extensively on topics related to marriage and family life. In addition to writing and lecturing, they have spent many years working with young couples in marriage enrichment groups. Both have been university professors and deans. Each now holds the position of Research Professor at U.S. International University. Bob is also an ordained minister. They live in San Diego, California, where they rejoice in their marriage, their three children, and their five grandchildren.

The Scripture quotations contained in this publication are from the New Revised Standard Version Bible, Copyright © 1989 by the Division of Christian Education of the National Council of the Churches of Christ in the United States of America, and are used by permission. All rights reserved.

FaithHome for Parents provides the church community with resources to support families and help children *to increase their faith, confirm their hope, and perfect them in love.*

ISBN 0-687-04892-3

Notes

Notes

Notes